# STOURHEAD

# STOURHEAD

Stephen Anderton with Alan Power

 National Trust

First published in the United Kingdom in 2019 by
National Trust Books
43 Great Ormond Street
London WC1N 3HZ
An imprint of Pavilion Books Company Ltd

ISBN: 9781911358596

A CIP catalogue record for this book is available from the
British Library.

25 24 23 22 21 20 19
10 9 8 7 6 5 4 3 2 1

Reproduction by Rival Colour Ltd, UK
Printed and bound by 1010 Printing International Ltd, China

This book can be ordered direct from the publisher at the website:
www.pavilionbooks.com, or try your local bookshop.

PREVIOUS PAGE Stourhead's grounds are picture perfect and visited by
thousands each year, but who designed them, and what kind of lives did
they lead?

RIGHT The High Cross was brought from Bristol and reassembled here by
the Palladian bridge to represent northern, gothic architecture, in contrast
to so many Classical buildings. Its delicate detailing has required frequent
major repair and stabilisation over the centuries.

# Contents

# Foreword

Almost three hundred years ago, a revolution was underway on these islands like no other. The aesthetic appreciation of nature was on the ascendance and experience of landscape was becoming fashionable.

French and Dutch formal gardens gave way to a desire for more rustic, natural styles. Landscape and gardens were celebrated in poetry, painting and literature, helping to develop new ideas about gardens and how they should be experienced. Added to this mix came a flourishing of the arts and culture in Georgian society. Alongside the aristocracy and landed gentry, a new professional class of bankers, merchants and entrepreneurs undertook Grand Tours of continental Europe. Their quest was to see first hand the romantic ruins of lost civilisations in Italy and Greece and to absorb the lessons of classical literature.

All this fuelled a revolution in garden design and the emergence of a new style, the Landscape Garden, an idealised version of the classical world transported to the soft, verdant rolling landscape of England.

This was a peculiarly British art form but, unlike art, it was not just for looking at. This was to be an immersive experience, a journey of the senses, discovering a series of vistas and views, each designed to generate different emotional responses.

Of all the great landscape gardens created during the eighteenth century, Stourhead, begun in the 1740s, stands out. No other garden from this period feels as complete, so perfectly balanced in its ideas, design and execution, and in the intensity of feeling it induces.

The story of Stourhead is a fascinating one, as much about the people who created it, as the garden itself. Who better to tell that story than one of the country's leading garden authors, Stephen Anderson, and Stourhead's Head Gardener, Alan Power?

Stephen explores successive generations of the Hoare family, their impact on Stourhead and how the garden changed and developed from a private realm to one attracting over half a million visitors a year.

Alan takes us on a journey around the garden, focusing on its remarkable collection of plants, not least its magnificent trees, reminding us at every turn that Stourhead is a living work of art.

Whether you've visited Stourhead many times or have never been, this book is an informative companion to one of Britain's greatest gardens.

MIKE CALNAN
HEAD OF GARDENS, NATIONAL TRUST

RIGHT The small islands in the lake stand barely above water level, allowing the trees on them to seem almost to float upon the water.

# Introduction

Great houses and gardens are all about people. They are an autobiography in three dimensions – in the case of Stourhead, an autobiography of the Hoare family. Over 240 years, the Hoare banking dynasty developed this extraordinary icon of English culture, influenced by the lives and ideas and the politics and fashions that guided them, and recognised internationally even from its earliest days. And, for the last 70 years, Stourhead has been in the care of the National Trust.

It has been a story of continuous development over that time. Yet, one generation will possess talents and interests that do not mesh with what has been achieved by their predecessors, and every family can have its black sheep. One generation may be extravagant innovators, and the next merely (but invaluably) a safe pair of hands, aware of their personal limitations but intent on repair and consolidation. There may also be periods of benign neglect. Yet overall, a project may prosper, not least if it has plenty of money behind it as Stourhead usually did.

Never forget that a great house and garden, however large, is still someone's home, whether as an infant, a newly-wed or a widow, and is lived in and cherished as only a private home can be. What's more, a new house and garden are a flight of fancy, an opportunity to indulge in so many fields of creativity, from art and architecture to the commissioning of superb paintings

RIGHT The western, rear façade of the house, largely Edwardian, looks over parkland to a stone obelisk topped with a golden disc. The Gallery wing stands to the left, Library to the right.

and furniture and the planting of trees. They are an expression of one's intellect and taste, one's sense of fun, and of the joys and sadnesses that shape the mind. An autobiography indeed.

No artistic endeavour is entirely original, whatever a creator or critic may claim; it is always built upon the ideas and traditions that educated and influenced the artist. Stourhead, both house and garden, were not uniquely original, but they did embody the new eighteenth-century fashions for Palladian architecture and landscape gardening that were then emerging in England. Other men of means were playing the same game – Charles Hamilton at Painshill, Lord Cobham at Stowe, and William Shenstone at The Leasowes – but Stourhead is one of the earliest and most successful hands to be played in the game of landscape gardening. It is probably the world's best known and best loved.

All credit goes to the determination of those players, too, for theirs was a long game where elements such as trees could take a hundred years to develop and fully shape the garden. What optimism for life and the future was there, in a period when, for the rich as for the poor, there were no antibiotics or anaesthetics and infant mortality was desperately high. All credit to the Hoares for their ambitions, for they were not aristocrats from a long-privileged and powerful family, but new men, of the kind whose money came from industry or trade. For a man of commerce, aspiring to political influence and a place in high society, a house and garden and country estate – *land* – showed he was part of the establishment, a family of power. Some new men merely bought their showpiece estates and had them made through the reliable hands of famous, fashionable designers; others, like the Hoares, took delight in creating their own vision and themselves setting the fashion.

The world was a smaller place then. Those men with the passion of the Enlightenment – intellectual men of science and art and literature in the late seventeenth and eighteenth century – were brought together through the learned societies. They knew who else was making ambitious gardens or amassing collections of art or antiquities, and they shared ideas. It was an exciting time to be at work.

Such excitement could take different forms. For some people it was the creation in their gardens of images reminiscent of the Roman *campagna*, complete with the classical ruined temples that they had seen on their Grand Tours of Europe, or of a landscape alluding to literary or political themes. But still, whatever the *raison d'être* of the garden, more often than not the temples and monuments in English Landscape Gardens were not ruined like the ancient ones seen in Syria, Greece and Italy. Instead they were new, perfect, and surrounded not by hot, dry woods and hills, but by green, rolling English landscape, clean and spacious. It was an image not so much of the loss of antique civilisation as a celebration of it in perfect condition, an image suggesting the best of the past was here being re-created in a modern Britain. And if the Palladian house echoed ancient and Renaissance Italy, in the garden the whole world could be laid out: there might be buildings in Turkish, Chinese and Egyptian styles, as well as European

Gothic, classical and rustic. Some might even call it cultural appropriation.

That unlikely but confident combination of classical architecture set in a green northern setting gives delight today to people from many cultures. The image of the Stourhead Pantheon, seen across the lake from the arched Palladian Bridge, is famous the world over, at home on jigsaws, biscuit tins, t-shirts and tea towels just as much as in learned journals of art, garden and architectural history.

That image of Italy in verdant rural England went on to inspire the so-called 'English garden' – *le jardin Anglais* – throughout the world, and it still does. In 1830s Britain it formed the basis of the first public recreational spaces, such as Birkenhead Park in Merseyside, which in turn were the inspiration for Central Park in New York. In the middle of the twentieth century, Nikolaus Pevsner, the celebrated art and architectural historian, claimed that the Landscape Garden was arguably Britain's greatest contribution to the visual arts, and he may be right. The Landscape Garden is one of Britain's most successful exports and Stourhead continues to play a huge part in that success.

RIGHT What looks like a river entering the lake is one of Stourhead's delightful visual tricks – the water is merely a small wing of the lake.

# Stourhead House and Gardens

## KEY

**1** House
**2** Obelisk
**3** St Peter's Pump
**4** Grotto
**5** Gothic Cottage
**6** Pantheon
**7** Temple of Apollo
**8** Palladian Bridge
**9** Temple of Flora
**10** Bristol Cross
**11** St Peter's Church

# The Early Years

## *(1648–1725)*

# Sir Richard Hoare (1648–1718)

Standing in the presence of any magnificent house and garden, a visitor is, at some point, likely to wonder, where did the *money* come from? How was it that such colossal sums were available? At Stourhead the answer is simple: banking. And the man who, from humble beginnings and from scratch began the bank, was Richard Hoare (1648–1718). Stourhead owes everything to him. It was his industry and passionate work ethic that provided the funds for his son Henry 'the Good' (1677–1725) to build Stourhead.

Richard Hoare's father was a successful horse-dealer but apprenticed Richard (one of his 17 children) to a London goldsmith at the age of 17. His abilities and promise must have been considerable because by the time he was 24 (in 1672) he had bought out his master's business and set up Hoare's Bank in Cheapside. In 1690 he moved it to prestigious new premises on Fleet Street where a golden bottle, hanging over the entrance, marked its presence to the world. The bank remains there to this day.

The leap from goldsmith to banker may seem a big one to us now, but it was then a practical progression. Fleet Street was part-house, part-workshop and part-safety vault: customers would bring precious metals and gems for repair and money would be borrowed or deposited with the bank. Richard was, in effect, a pawnbroker and money-lender to the members of high society (the term 'bank' only came into use around 1700). Most of his lending was to only 20 members of the aristocracy.

Business thrived despite unexpected competition from a newly formed Bank of England, a private company set up to handle national debt in 1694. Richard was knighted by Queen Anne on her accession to the throne in 1702, the same year that his son Henry married and became Partner in the business. Richard's industry made his position in London ever greater, becoming an Alderman of the City of London, a Member of Parliament and finally, in 1712, Lord Mayor of London, Europe's biggest capital city. Not bad going for a horse-trader's son.

Perhaps the family's interest in gardening was already present in Richard, because he asked his sons, working abroad in Amsterdam and Genoa, to supply him with interesting plants: 'Good flowers (except toolips) that will blow this year or next without faile.'

Within 52 years he had risen to become a wealthy man with connections to the all-important rich aristocracy. It was his son Henry, then living over the shop with his wife and parents, who would drive the family's social position yet higher.

PREVIOUS PAGE Stourhead as it stands today, an eighteenth-century Palladian mansion with sympathetic early nineteenth-century wings, facing east to the downs across the park. A mid-nineteenth century park rail separates the animals from the lawn.

RIGHT Sir Richard Hoare (1648–1718), founder of Hoare's Bank, shown here as Lord Mayor of London in 1712, painted by Jonathan Richardson.

19

# Good Henry (1677–1725)

Richard's son, Henry, was given the nickname 'Good Henry' by his friends because of his philanthropic gestures, not least his contribution to the founding in 1719 of Westminster Hospital, 'for relieving the sick and needy'. Henry was familiar with human suffering, and was himself survived by only two sons and three daughters from his 11 children.

But he could afford to be generous. His share of bank profits was large, and the bank made good money (£28,000, a huge sum at the time) from dealings with the South Sea Company. In 1711 the company had been given a monopoly of trade with South America by the government, and was soon to collapse spectacularly in the financial disaster (for some) known as the South Sea Bubble of 1720. One of its victims was John Aislabie, Chancellor of the Exchequer, who retired disgraced from public life to his home in Yorkshire where he made the fine semi-formal landscape garden at Studley Royal.

The Hoares were now a seriously wealthy clan with Richard, his son Henry and grandson Henry, all living above the premises in Fleet Street. Good Henry saw the opportunity to elevate his family's place in society by buying a country estate and effectively becoming part of the landed gentry. To that end in 1717 he bought for £23,000 (a vast sum) the Manor of Stourton in Wiltshire, home of the Stourton family since medieval times. The property was now for sale as a result of debt and damage during the Civil War (1642–51) that had raged across the country when his father Richard was only a small child.

How could he best use the new estate to establish the family's social standing? Henry decided he would knock down the war-torn ancient Stourton House and build a new one in the very latest fashion, and for this he must choose an architect. If it was a blow that his father Richard had died shortly after the purchase of the estate, at least he was now senior partner in the bank so wealthier still, and his own second son, another Henry, was a healthy teenager.

It was a time of great change in architectural style in Britain. Palladianism was to be the new fashion and Henry liked the idea. Most conspicuously Richard Boyle, Lord Burlington, would design and build Chiswick House copying Palladio's Villa Capra at Vicenza; Chiswick remains today perhaps the best-known example of strict 1720s Palladianism.

ABOVE Chiswick House, Lord Burlington's Palladian villa in West London, begun 1725, was built as a suite for entertaining rather than a complete dwelling house. It is grand yet surprisingly compact, and a landmark in English architectural style.

LEFT 'Good Henry' was so-named for his philanthropy, including his contribution to the founding of Westminster Hospital in 1719. The gothic hospital was built in 1834 opposite Westminster Abbey.

Andrea Palladio (1508–1580) was a Venetian architect who set out to reinterpret for contemporary living the classical architecture of ancient Rome, as had been set out long ago by the Roman architect Vitruvius. Palladio published his ideas in *The Four Books of Architecture* (1570), extolling the use of symmetry, good proportion, clarity, order, classical decorative motifs, and, most familiar to us today, the pedimented temple front. Many of Palladio's beautifully proportioned villas still stand today, in the Veneto region of northern Italy.

Britain first began to employ Palladian architecture during the time of Inigo Jones (1573–1652) who was the architect of London's Somerset House, the Banqueting House at Whitehall (in front of which King Charles I would be beheaded in 1649) and the National Maritime Museum, Greenwich.

LEFT *Good Henry* (1677–1725) by Michael Dahl. Henry purchased the Stourton estate in 1717 and commissioned Colen Campbell to design a new mansion, to be called Stourhead; the plan can be seen in his hand. Henry died before the house was completed.

RIGHT (FROM TOP TO BOTTOM) Stourhead's 1721 south front with Campbell's original steps descending into the garden; Campbell's final design for Houghton Hall, Norfolk. 1722; Campbell's original plan for Stourhead's eastern entrance front. The central portico was omitted by Henry and only completed in the late 1820s; Campbell's original design for Wanstead House, Surrey. 1715.

Sir Christopher Wren later assumed Jones's mantle as Surveyor General to the crown. It was Wren who, after the Great Fire of 1666, built so many city churches and St Paul's Cathedral. When Wren died, the job passed, briefly and without much success, to William Benson. Benson's sister, Jane, had married Good Henry, and his Deputy was the young Scottish architect Colen Campbell. Benson had built Wilbury House in Wiltshire (about 1710), perhaps the first truly Palladian house in Britain but it was to Campbell, not Benson, that Henry turned for his new house. Campbell and Lord Burlington would go on to become the great pioneers of Palladian architecture in Britain.

The house was to be built a few fields south of the now demolished Stourton House, overlooking the six springs where the River Stour started, and to be named Stourhead. Campbell's plan for Stourhead, loosely based on Palladio's Villa Emo near Fanzolo di Vedelago, was later published in a volume of Campbell's hugely influential *Vitruvius Britannicus*, which displayed the new Palladian architecture of Britain (Henry already owned the first Volume, of 1715.) It was, in effect, a British answer to Palladio's *Four Books of Architecture*. Campbell's plan can be identified in Michael Dahl's painting of Henry, standing proud and grandly bewigged with it scrolled in his hand. Master builder Nathaniel Ireson set to work in 1719 and Stourhead began to rise.

By 1725, when Stourhead was completed, Campbell was building other great houses in strict Palladian style, notably Wanstead House in Surrey (1722, loosely based on John Webb's Amesbury Abbey, 1661) and Mereworth Castle in Kent (1723); for Lord Burlington he had built Burlington House on Piccadilly, now the Royal Academy. Sir Robert Walpole had begun his palatial Houghton Hall, Norfolk, in 1722.

But Stourhead was to be a villa, a large and luxurious country house rather than a palace, and it was perhaps this wish for simplicity and the pastoral idyll of the wise politician-turned-farmer that persuaded Henry to omit Campbell's proposed grand portico over the entrance on the eastern front. Perhaps he felt a less grand appearance was more appropriate, something more akin to Stourhead's cleaner garden front on the south side.

Perhaps he felt that the looming shadow created by a grand portico would have been more welcoming and attractive in a hot Mediterranean climate than in cooler England. It has been wisely suggested by the designer Penelope Hobhouse that in the Moorish tradition in hot-climate gardens, it is the habit to sit in the shade and look out into the sunny parts of a garden, whereas in Britain we prefer to sit in the warm sun and look into the garden's enticing shady vistas.

Whatever Henry's reasoning, the result was an elegantly simple square house, of beautifully proportioned rooms just like Villa Emo's, the Entrance Hall a perfect 9m (30ft) cube with a proposed chapel to match at the rear of the house, and a staircase forming the central core of the house. Outside, a flight of steps rose grandly to the front door and two smaller flights led to a central door on the south side of the house facing the garden. The principal rooms were on a raised main floor, the piano nobile, with domestic offices in the basement and one floor of bedrooms above, the whole edifice topped with garrets to house the servants hidden from the outside behind a parapet. It was a cool, masculine building.

A grand State Bedroom was made for the grandest visitors, or in case visiting royalty should require it (they never did). So proud was Henry of acquiring the Pope's Cabinet on his travels that he devoted a whole room to it. This fabulously ornate piece of furniture was made in around 1585 for Pope Sixtus V, a member of the Italian Peretti family. The last member of the Peretti line became a nun, who left the cabinet to her convent, which then sold it to Henry. It consists of a tall, church-like façade in African blackwood (reminiscent of the Duomo in Siena) covered in *pietre dure* work in semi-precious stones, with 150 drawers inside.

The cost of building Stourhead was £10,000, a vast fortune in today's money. Henry would have been very proud of it had he not died aged 47 just as it was being completed. Still, he must have gone to his tomb in the vault beneath nearby Stourton church knowing that his 19-year-old son Henry was alive and healthy, and there to take over from him, both at the bank and in the completion of his great family project.

ABOVE The Pope's Cabinet, a precious and fantastic creation of 1585 in wood and semi-precious stones, brought back from Italy erected upon a grand plinth.

LEFT The Entrance Hall, with family portraits, looking through the central stairwell to the Saloon. Stourhead was renowned from the start for being a comfortably warm house.

# The Road to Paradise

My yearning for the outdoors probably runs through my veins; it is in my genes. Generations of the family on my mother's side have worked close to nature. Her passion for plants and gardens began when she was a child and I believe that her love for gardening grew out of a childhood relationship with the countryside. It is her way of having a little of that magic with her every day.

There are several things that fill my soul with delight, but the view from a hillside out to the sea is certainly close to the top of the list. Another is the view from the Pantheon at Stourhead across the lake early in the morning as the sun rises to be greeted by the landscape.

I grew up in the Irish city of Cork and my first efforts at gardening came about in a slightly strange way. My mum and dad announced that we were selling our house and moving to another part of Cork; a larger property and a bigger garden was the plan. The hunt began for a suitable house, but the real objective for mum was the garden: ideally south-facing, much bigger and with the space for a seating area where we could all share in the joy she got from it. Eventually the deal was done and we moved. However, we didn't just pack the house, we packed the garden too. We took most of the plants with us and I was the master of the spade. I dug and potted, divided and rearranged the whole garden ready for its new life with us. It was an amazing time, I loved the work, enjoyed seeing the calluses develop on my hands. Seeing the stains of a day's efforts on my palms and the ache of hard work as I fell asleep somehow made me feel complete. That was it – I wanted to be a gardener.

Coincidentally, a chap who lived close to my mother's sister was just that. He was a gardener who had recently returned from the UK having studied horticulture and was setting up on his own; there was an opportunity on the horizon. The gardener's name was Billy Irwin and

LEFT Spring flowers bloom cheerfully in front of the gardener's mess room at Stourhead.

he gave me a job working as his help for the summer. He was based nearly 18km (11 miles) from where we lived so it was a long cycle ride every morning, but it was worth it. We gardened various properties towards East Cork and some right on the coast with views to the sea; I was on the brink of a huge personal voyage of discovery.

I submitted my application for Writtle College near Chelmsford in Essex to begin my studies in September 1990. Horticulture is a massive subject, and it keeps growing, if you will excuse the pun. There were sessions on commercial horticulture, growing plants and vegetables for sale; there were plant-science sessions where we experimented with the effects of the different zones of the light spectrum on plant growth; and there were visits off-campus to different places – nurseries, cricket grounds, Wimbledon – but there was one where I could have stayed indefinitely – Marks Hall Gardens and Arboretum in Coggleshall.

The curator, Jonathan Jukes, was a past pupil of the college and took us on a tour of the grounds together with his dog Rosie. I was captivated by what he had to say, by his obvious love for the place, and by everything I saw that day.

It was fascinating to see the trees in this very functional and almost nurturing setting. At this point my understanding of coniferous plantations was that they were primarily a financial operation: a relatively sterile, uninviting monocrop environment. Jonathan put paid to all of that with tales of a goshawk having been spotted on the estate, as well as a buzzard (rare at the time), bullfinches in abundance, a variety of owls, and an amazingly diverse population of butterflies on the long grassy sheltered rides between the compartments of trees.

Emerging from the trees, we came upon a junction of rides – five or six, like the spokes of a wheel – and arrived at heart of the forest. I had never seen or felt anything like this before. Jonathan had chosen an ingenious route and saved the best until last. A gigantic oak tree stood before me, massive in every way; its trunk was so thick that I lost my sense of scale and perspective for a moment and felt as if I was getting smaller. A single trunk, some 10m (33ft) in circumference, at my chest height divided into tree-like, muscular limbs at around 4m (13ft) from the ground and formed its own, elevated woodland full of ferns, lichens, creatures and insects. I was silent but spinning. This nearly 800-year-old tree was magnificent and I was privileged to be here.

Things happen for a reason and sometimes it is worth slowing down to consider them all. I managed to get a job at Marks Hall as part of my work experience and after graduation I carried on working there. I was hungry to learn more and Jonathan encouraged me to study Arboriculture as I had an obvious interest in the tree collection we were planting and managing at the Arboretum. I headed to Merrist Wood, the home of Arboriculture at the time, and combined my studies there with some work at the Arboretum.

I would always keep half an eye on the jobs that were being advertised around the UK, and in particular with the National Trust. And suddenly there it was, the advert I had been waiting for: Gardener Arborist for the National Trust at Stourhead in Wiltshire.

In early December 1995 I was called to Stourhead by Head Gardener Peter Hall for an interview. I had the

RIGHT Stunning rural scenery was the foundation for my road into gardening. Picture perfect, the plants drew me in and I was hooked.

day before to acquaint myself with the garden and be wowed by the place even in winter.

I can still recall my garden walk that day: it was a chilly, overcast day and I had time to kill. As an enthusiastic mountaineer and tree-climber I was initially interested in seeing the giants that populated the landscape. Purposefully walking from tree to tree, I would identify them on my approach from their form, leaf shape, foliage colour, size and every other detail I could use as a clue. The trees were huge, towering specimens and my natural reaction was to reach out and place my hand on each trunk to make my acquaintance with them, a little sign of respect. Having walked around the entire garden, examined all the trees that drew my eye, admired the specimens and taken pride in my identification of the rarer ones, I thought I was done. Dwarfed by the rugged limbs of a 200-year-old tulip tree my gaze fell on the reflection in the lake of the Pantheon on the bank opposite: clearly there was another layer of this garden that was craving my admiration. I had been infatuated with the tree collection and had merely glanced at the views, missing the essence of this paradise. I removed the crumpled garden map from my pocket and planned another route of exploration. I had not yet seen the house and its grounds so I headed off to discover its mysteries. It turned out the gates were locked for the winter, but this was not to stop an experienced tree-climber from getting in to have a peek.

LEFT Under beech trees, Stourhead's many acres of laurel lawn so favoured by Colt Hoare, today cut by machine, make areas impenetrable but add a wonderful glitter to the forest floor.

I can still feel the way the anticipation built as I walked along the path that led from the house into the shade of the trees. The openness of the lawns and the expanse of winter sky were compressed as the trees and shrubs enveloped the area and channelled my progress in a very definite direction. Then my progress was stopped, like a red light stops the traffic with complete authority. The Temple of Apollo was framed by the trees on a distant hillside, standing powerfully above the garden and protected on three sides by obedient plantations of naked beech trees. It all began to make sense as a garden. I continued on my stealthy journey on the forbidden paths and the garden unfolded through a series of perfect framed views worthy of any Italian rural landscape. Lost in the moments I was experiencing, I had completely forgotten the reason for this pleasurable stroll – the interview was getting closer every minute.

To this day, I don't know how I managed to string together an articulate sentence. I answered questions and we chatted about the place, the role, the trees and shrubs, a little history and my desire to work there. I remember the moment during one of my answers when Peter lifted his head to listen more intently to my description of the difference between Stourhead and an Arboretum. I used the word 'picturesque' in relation to the distribution of plants in the garden at Stourhead and spoke of the botanical importance of a plant being equal to its placement and position within the overall designed landscape.

Peter called me by 11 am the following day; the job was mine and I accepted without hesitation. I was young and I was enchanted with the place.

# Henry the Magnificent

## (1705–1785)

# A Dutiful Son

Richard's grandson Henry – later fondly titled Henry the Magnificent as his father had been Good Henry – spent much of his youth at Quarley, near Andover in Hampshire, another of his father's properties, and he had enjoyed his hunting and drinking as much as the next young man. On his father's death, however, he behaved like the dutiful son, helping his mother to manage the house and estate at Stourhead where she now permanently resided, her husband having left it to her for her lifetime. The two of them spent the next 16 years completing and furnishing the house, whereupon, at her death Henry moved into Stourhead. Inevitably he and his mother made changes to Campbell's original vision for the house, not least in the use and purpose of the various rooms. In particular, Campbell had planned a Chapel at the rear of the house, another 9m (30ft) cube to balance the Entrance Hall at the front; however, this was now extended beyond the line of Campbell's original back wall to make a much longer room, a saloon, which would also serve as a grand dining room.

## The Making of the Man

Young Henry's private and public life had moved far ahead by the time he inherited Stourhead. In 1726, after his father's death, he had made an advantageous marriage to Anne, daughter of Lord and Lady Masham. Abigail Masham was appointed Keeper of the Privy Purse to Queen Anne in 1711 and her connections brought important custom to Hoare's Bank. But he must have been devastated when his new wife died following complications after giving birth to a daughter (Ann, who would herself die in 1735 at the age of eight).

It was important that Henry the Magnificent should produce a male heir to inherit Stourhead and he quickly married again, this time to the heiress Susanna Colt. Through the 1730s they had three children, the first fortunately a boy (another Henry, of course) and then two daughters, Susanna and Anne.

With his duty done, so to speak, Henry the Magnificent spent much of 1739–41 abroad in Paris and Rome, buying Old Master paintings of the seventeenth and eighteenth centuries and shipping them back to add to his collection of work of the highest quality that included canvases by Nicolas Poussin, Gaspard Dughet, Carlo Maratta, Richard Wilson and William Hoare of Bath (no relation).

The decade also saw Henry become Member of Parliament for Salisbury (1734–41). As senior partner in the bank he was now entitled to take half its annual profits and was owner of several properties in London.

PREVIOUS PAGE The Palladian Bridge with the Pantheon behind. The scene is much more enclosed than in Henry the Magnificent's day, for his was an open landscape where sheep grazed right up to the house.

RIGHT Henry the Magnificent (1705–1785) by Michael Dahl and John Wootton, horse painter. Henry created the bones of the landscape garden, of lakes and temples and bridges, which his successors then embellished with more exotic planting.

ABOVE Apart from garden buildings, water and greenery were Henry's only tools in the creation of his landscape garden. And light, of course: bright sunlight, shadows and reflection.

LEFT Henry Hoare loved the greens of the beech leaves at Stourhead. His beloved beech trees thrive around the grounds and were a major part of the initial planting that framed the garden.

He had also acquired his uncle William Benson's nearby Wilbury House, in 1734. It was through Benson that Henry met many of the artists and designers who would help him with his own great project at Stourhead: Henry Flitcroft who would be the architect for the garden temples, John Michael Rysbrack and John Cheere who would create statues and plasterwork, and John Wootton, one of England's up-and-coming painters from whom Henry bought several canvases.

He began to develop gardens around the house. Stretching away on its south side, as a pleasure ground for his mother, was a long semi-circular lawn, possibly walled, and ending in a statue of Apollo. At right angles to this he made a Fir Walk, an avenue of tall conifers leading to a ride of lush, soft turf along the top of a high ridge from which there were wonderful views across his estates and four counties.

Stourhead was a garden of greens, a preference that remained close to Henry's heart throughout his life. As he put it, 'The greens should be ranged together in large masses as the shades are in a painting: to contrast the dark masses with light ones, and to relieve each dark mass itself with little sprinklings of lighter greens here and there.' He would have been happy only planting his beloved beech and firs.

But after Henry's mother Jane died in 1741, good times turned sour once more. His second wife Susanna died two years later, leaving him with three young children to bring up alone. Would he marry a third time? His decision was no. He had his heir Henry, now 13, and with fresh determination his mind turned to ideas of gardening, the project that would occupy the rest of his life.

# The Early Landscapers

Henry came to gardening at a moment of great change, as the fashion moved from the formality of the Baroque to the early landscape gardens of the 1720s and 1730s, which were indeed landscape gardens of grass and trees and water but, drawing on their Baroque antecedents, were laid out formally and more geometrically than later landscape gardens. Britain was developing a hybrid style of its own.

As early as the 1710s the landscaper and ex-soldier Charles Bridgeman had been making a geometric landscape of grand canals, *allées* and bastions for Lord Cobham at Stowe. Bridgeman was followed by the painter and landscaper William Kent whose assistant, latterly, was Lancelot 'Capability' Brown. Kent began to soften Bridgeman's design, introducing curves and naturalism where all had previously been straight. The Elysian Fields were Kent's greatest contribution to Stowe: a small, meandering valley where three temples – to Ancient Virtue, Modern Virtue and the British Worthies – played with Lord Cobham's opinions on the current state of politics, Whigs (liberals) versus Tories and the Crown. It was a new kind of garden, of narrative and of allusion, a game for the intellect. A roofed Palladian bridge cemented the stylistic link between house and garden and became one of the icons of eighteenth-century gardening (there are two matching bridges, at Wilton House, Wiltshire, and Prior Park, Bath).

Even the garden of Wanstead, the Palladian house of 1722 created by Colen Campbell, had been modernised. From geometric beginnings designed by George London, one of the last great formalist designers, Wanstead had been transformed by 1736. As English antiquarian John Loveday wrote in that year, 'The Garden just in view from the house is truly wild and Rural, a very spacious Lawn before the house Woods about it – Water at the bottom of the view; the River runs through the Water. Here are some fine Walks under Arbours of Trees, Statues placed in other parts. Woods and River bound one side of the Garden, a fine prospect of woody Countrey every way.' It could almost be a description of Henry's garden-to-be at Stourhead.

The world of garden landscaping has always been deliciously and competitively close. Garden makers knew about the other ambitious competitors and the fashions of the day. The banking business, too, meant Henry was in touch with those makers and shakers of the day who, with land and income to play with, shared his interest in gardens. The world was a smaller place than today.

In 1729 John Aislabie, disgraced after his part in the financial debacle that was the South Sea Bubble, retreated to Yorkshire where he started work on his semi-formal water garden and landscape at Studley Royal, Ripon. One might compare the more recent example of the way Sir Michael Heseltine dedicated himself to his famous garden at Thenford having abandoned the government of Margaret Thatcher

RIGHT Stowe's Palladian Bridge of 1738, inspired by its 1737 twin at Wilton House, Wiltshire.

over the Westland Affair in 1986. Such is the consolation of 'making places', as Capability Brown described gardening. It was Aislabie whose influence had helped William Benson to succeed Sir Christopher Wren as Surveyor General. It was a small world indeed.

Those early landscapers, Lord Burlington of Chiswick House and the Hon. Charles Hamilton of Painshill Park, both banked with Hoare's. Chiswick, on the outskirts of London, was begun as an artistic joint venture between Lord Burlington and William Kent. They had met in Italy while Burlington was touring Italy and Kent was working in Rome as a dealer in paintings for the English market. Rather like a student gap year, the eighteenth-century Grand Tour was meant to be an education in life for young gentlemen of means. They would travel to Italy via Paris, taking in the sights of Renaissance Florence and antiquities of ancient Rome, and perhaps travelling on to Greece. A letter of introduction to the great and good of a foreign city usually produced accommodation and suitably intelligent and wealthy company of similar social standing.

But if the Grand Tour became a chance for young men to misbehave away from the strictures of polite society at home, it was also for the serious-minded a chance to study the great art of the European tradition and to demonstrate their good taste by collecting works of the Old Masters of Italian painting from the seventeenth century, most famously the landscape paintings of Nicolas Poussin (1594–1665) and Claude Lorrain (c.1604–82) or Henry's favourite Gaspard Dughet (1615–75).

The poet Alexander Pope played a vital role in launching this new landscape movement and his verse letter of 1731, the *Epistle of Lord Burlington*, set out what were to be the founding principles of landscape gardeners. Henry wrote himself that it is the habit

'of looking into books and the pursuit of knowledge which distinguishes only the gentleman from the vulgar'. He knew some of the *Epistle* by heart:

> To build, to plant, whatever you intend,
> To rear the column, or the Arch to bend,
> To swell the Terras, or to sink the Grot;
> In all, let Nature never be forgot.
> But treat the Goddess like a modest fair,
> Nor over-dress, nor leave her wholly bare;
> Let not each beauty ev'ry where be spy'd,
> Where half the skill is decently to hide.
> He gains all points, who pleasingly confounds,
> Surprises, varies and conceals the Bounds.
>
> Consult the Genius of the Place in all;
> That tells the Waters or to rise, or fall,
> Or help th'ambitious Hill the heaven to scale,
> Or scoops in circling theatres the Vale,
> Calls in the Country, catches opening glades,
> Joins willing woods, and varies shades from shades,
> Now breaks or now directs, th' intending Lines:
> Paint as you plant, and, as you work, designs.

Such was the spirit of adventure in the gardening world when Henry set to work.

LEFT What was the genius of the place – the *spirit* – that ultimately inspired Stourhead? It must be the seven springs which combine to form Henry's shallow 6ha (15 acre) lake, one of them commanded by the River God and water nymph in Henry's waterside Grotto. Steep valley sides create powerful contrasts of light and shade when the sun is low.

43

# A Scheme for Henry's Garden

By 1735, Henry's mother had gone, and his first wife and daughter. He was about to start his garden in earnest, provoked by the spirit of the times and his extraordinary wealth. An obvious question is, was there a grand plan from the start? It seems not.

Probably the idea of a garden circuit appealed, as did the idea of making his garden around water. In Barratt and Son's *Description of Stourhead* (1818) it is clearly announced that 'in perambulating any extensive demesne, some regular order of progress should be laid down. From a perfect knowledge of the grounds at Stourhead, we are persuaded that such an arrangement is absolutely necessary, in order to show the place to greatest advantage.'

Henry set out to make a garden of classical allusions in the same way as Kent and Lord Cobham at Stowe. But this was not to be a political garden with an axe to grind. Henry was a banker, after all, not a politician, and as a businessman it was in his interest to be acceptable to all his customers whatever their political persuasion. This was to be a garden of a simpler kind, a game of aesthetics, of poetics, not argument.

It is too easy, however, to see Henry's allusory landscape of water and temples as the only garden at Stourhead, as *the* garden. In fact, what he had created by the time of his death was a garden in three contrasting parts, of which the landscape garden was only one. They were only fully appreciated if one were living there in the house and able to choose from there which way to go, or how to lead one's visitors to entertain them best. If these three parts are seen as separate entities, it gives a proper context to the landscape of temples and water.

LEFT The tulip tree, *Liriodendron tulipifera*, is so named for its large but inconspicuous white and orange flowers, but is planted mostly for its autumn colour. It comes from the eastern seaboard of North America, from Nova Scotia to Florida, and was already in British gardens by 1688.

## 1. Around the House

Like Capability Brown in his landscapes of the second half of the eighteenth century, Henry made the approach to his house through simple parkland, the drive curling round to a flight of stone steps to the front door on the east side, from where there was a 180-degree view of the chalk downs. Farm animals grazed close to the house: it was a thoroughly pastoral, elegant scene. John Dryden's translations of the works of Virgil (1697) and of the *Aeneid* especially, were then popular classics and had helped to establish the fashion for the bucolic. Such texts would have been a solid part of Henry's education.

On the south side, a double flight of steps led down from the house, this time into a level enclosed lawn several times the size of the building.

## 2. The Terrace Ride

Stourhead house stands on the lip of a long, north–south ridge. It was on this line, nearest the house, that Henry had made his Fir Walk in the 1730s, in effect, launching a 3.2km (2 mile) Terrace ride to the highest point in the landscape, from which one could see the world for a fair distance around. If the garden around the house was a social space, this was a place for invigorating exercise and a sense of dominion over the landscape below.

## 3. The Landscape Garden

In contrast to the first two parts of the garden, the landscape garden sat in a valley entirely separated by trees from the house garden and the terrace. Only by stepping through those trees can one begin to see the

magical and intellectually provocative landscape down below. For someone approaching from the house now, the landscape garden is something surprising and sequestered. In Henry's day it must have been a complete revelation in every sense, stylistically astonishing, whereas today we are perfectly familiar with a landscape of water, trees and temples.

ABOVE Campbell's grand staircase rises from the gravel to a principal floor well above ground level (the piano nobile), providing commanding views over the parkland to the chalk downs beyond.

RIGHT In Henry's day, before the addition of the portico and flanking wings, the park and grazing animals came right up to the house. This was common practice in landscape gardens and placed the house at the centre of its rural and agricultural surroundings.

# A Tour of Henry's Completed Garden Then and Now

To descend the steps from the house on to that large open lawn must have felt like a moment of great calm, but to tempt his visitors forwards Henry placed a large statue of Apollo at the far end. Having arrived there, the fun could begin. And it was fun: all great gardens are a caprice, a serious delight to their creators, totally unnecessary, and extraordinarily pleasurable to make.

## A Gothic Tribute

From Apollo, Henry's Fir Walk of subtle greens proceeded northwards, and concluded with a 36.5m (120ft) stone obelisk topped by a gilded 1.8m (6ft) disk: the sun, whose god was Apollo. Beyond this stretched the long, verdant Terrace ride, which he closed in 1772 with a tall tower dedicated to King Alfred the Great. Apart from the trials of the weather and occasional encounters with lightning, and despite a tragic accident during the Second World War in which an American Airforce crew lost their lives (see page 146), the tower still stands in good order today. The return journey to the house passed *below* the ridge and was enlivened by the addition of two other architectural features: St Peter's Pump is a late fifteenth-century structure that had previously stood near St Peter's Church in Bristol, and was erected at Stourhead in 1768; and The Convent, a pretty little cottage, now privately occupied and not accessible to visitors, then occupied by a gamekeeper and his daughter.

The possible springboards to the creation of Alfred's Tower are many. At Painshill Park the Hon. Charles Hamilton was making a fine and ambitious landscape garden. He was a customer of the bank and Henry lent him £6,000 to make the garden until finally, too heavily in debt, Hamilton had to sell up and abandon his great project. (Painshill, almost derelict in 1970s and scarred by

LEFT  St Peter's Pump, one of Henry's pieces of architectural salvage, from Bristol, set up in 1768 in the shallow valley above the garden where the lake's waters rise.

RIGHT  King Alfred's Tower, of 1772, is triangular, it has been suggested, to offer less wind resistance. Three walls and a spiral stair of 225 steps enclose a hollow core open to the skies.

the M3 motorway, has been saved by a miraculous restoration and now stands as one of the great Landscape Gardens once again.) Hamilton had made a brick Gothic tower at the far end of his landscape walk. Not to be outdone, Henry gave up the idea of re-creating St Mark's Tower, Venice, and made his own brick tower; at 48.8m (160ft), it was three times as high as Hamilton's, hollow from top to bottom but with an interior staircase comprising 225 steps up to the roof.

At Stowe Lord Cobham had employed James Gibbs to make a Gothic Temple of Liberty which, in a garden where most other monuments were of pale classical ashlar, was of a contrasting brown stone in celebration of the cultural traditions and freedoms of Northern Europe facing interminable wars with the Catholic south. 'To the Liberties of our Ancestors' runs its dedication. Henry's tower was of red brick, an equally blunt colour enshrining blunt principles. Very curiously the Temple of Liberty was triangular, and so was Henry's tower, although it has been said that this was partly to reduce wind resistance.

Like Cobham's Gothic Temple, Henry's tower was a celebration of English independence in a war-torn world; George III had ascended the throne in 1760 and the Seven Years' War had ended in 1763. It was said that on this spot in AD878 King Alfred had raised his standard in a last battle against the invading Danes and at the base of the tower there is a bust of Alfred and a rather long dedication (in Latin) explaining his importance.

But if a visitor to Henry's garden did not take the Terrace ride from Apollo to Alfred and back again, there was the immediate option to descend into a serene and magical world of classical allusion, to the ideas represented in ancient Roman poetry and to images of the classical world seen in those seventeenth-century paintings. Like Rome, Britain was a growing international power and it was good to compare itself to Rome's Augustan age.

Henry's first offering to a visitor was a glimpse of Stourton village church where his father lay buried, followed by the distant Temple of Apollo. There was, as yet, no indication that this was a circuit walk or even of there being a lake below. But gradually, past other glimpsed temples, the path descended through trees to the water and at last a secret world opened out: of smooth grassy shores and a crisply curving water's edge; of lawns fit for nymphs to play on.

ABOVE A glimpse of Stourton church and the Spread Eagle Inn below the garden, this time framed by trees.

LEFT A celebration of English independence: Alfred's Tower features a statue of King Alfred who, it is said, battled invading Danes on the spot where the tower now stands.

## Reflections in the Lake

Henry made the 6ha (15-acre) lake in 1754 by damming two existing pools fed by the springs in Six Wells Bottom that are the start of the River Stour (it reaches the sea at Christchurch on the Dorset coast). It was a shallow lake, only a few feet deep in some places, punctuated by two small flat islands planted with shrubs that seem to float on the surface of the water. Shallow it may be, but the wide, still waters provide reflections of most of the garden's buildings and thereby suggest a depth not only to the water but to the valley itself.

To reach the other side of the lake on foot would have meant walking all the way around its head waters to where the stream was narrower, so instead Henry constructed a white bridge in Palladian style. It was not of the roofed variety that graced Stowe, but a single, high wooden arch, which certain visitors suggested was Chinese in style. According to some accounts, it was terrifying to cross its many rickety steps. The diary of Mrs Philip Lybbe Powys in 1776 said it was 'frightful' and that 'the idea of going over a kind of ladder … and seeing the water through at first looks formidable.' But then if the next part of the garden was intended to represent Stygian gloom, well, in classical mythology crossing the River Styx to the Underworld was not supposed to be easy.

Henry's technique in moving people around his garden was to let them have time by the water in the light, then move them back among the trees, to give variety to the journey. And now, with the bridge crossed, the path led into leafy gloom beyond which was the Grotto, where classical allusion is brought to the fore. Here the garden becomes even more a sophisticated game.

LEFT The original white Palladian bridge was dismantled by Richard Colt Hoare in the late eighteenth century (see page 96), although a representation of the bridge was constructed for a 'Stourhead Revisited' event.

RIGHT Henry's little 'floating' island shrubberies are today dominated by massive tulip trees planted at the turn of the twentieth century, exchanging cool distance for colourful immediacy.

## The House of the Nymph

Henry's Grotto (c.1748) was not like Hamilton's fairyland grotto, full of rare sparkling minerals dripping from the walls and ceiling. This was a simpler affair of heavily corrugated tufa rocks and pebblework, built together into a hovel that backed itself, half-buried, into the bank. To enter the Grotto felt like a turning away from the water, a descent into the underworld, and the entrance tunnel was extended by Henry in the 1770s to make the feeling of descent into subterranean gloom even greater. The Latin inscription over the entrance reads (in translation) 'Inside are sweet waters and seats of living rock – the house of the nymphs.' It is a quotation from the *Aeneid*, Virgil's story of Aeneas's journey home after the fall of Troy, in which he must visit the gloomy Underworld but is now sheltering in a cave near Carthage. The presence of such cultural references in the reality of the garden must have added a frisson of pleasure to any educated person's visit. Could the visitor translate the Latin? Was one sufficiently educated and cultivated to know the source of the quotation and see, in the sombre path which led up to this damp grotto, echoes of Aeneas' travails? It was indeed a game.

The tunnel leads gently down to the first dark chamber in which a sculpted Nymph of the Grotto by John Cheere lies curled chastely asleep. Here, a further inscription, at her feet, is taken from Alexander Pope's translation of a fifteenth-century Italian poem:

*Nymph of the grot these sacred springs I keep*
*And to the murmur of these waters sleep;*
*Ah! Spare my slumbers, gently tread the cave,*
*And drink in silence or in silence lave.*

But then, turning from the nymph, one sees through a craggy opening an almost water-level view across the lake, at the far side of which is the Tuscan Doric Temple of Flora, the fourteenth-century Stourton church, the Gothic Bristol High Cross (see page 70) and a five-arched bridge in a different Palladian style (this was copied from Leoni's *Architecture of A. Palladio*,

Book III of 1721, also the source for Henry's wooden arched bridge). Many a landscape garden would have elaborate set-piece views centred on a classical temple or ruined castle, or even both in the same eyeful if Gothic was in the far distance; but Henry dared to put classical and Gothic – Rome and Britain – close together in the same picture, each tradition equally worthy of respect. It is a haunting image, in many ways incongruous even today, but still beautifully composed so that its incongruities are wonderfully appealing.

In the Grotto's next chamber is a robust statue by John Cheere of a river god, representing both the

FAR LEFT Rough stone arches recede into the darkness of the hillside, enfolding John Cheere's sleeping nymph.

ABOVE Turn from the nymph and there is one of Stourhead's great views, the water brought close to the opening in the Grotto wall so that one feels almost to be surfacing from below the water. It is in complete contrast to the gloom of the sleeping nymph's pool – animated, sunny and colourful.

Roman River Tiber and the River Stour, one of whose springs issues below the statue. Again, to enhance the sense of damp seclusion, neither statue faces the view but looks inwards. Only the visitor can see out and appreciate the Grotto's relationship to the world.

The Grotto is left by means of a rocky stair until the path emerges into full light again and there looms the vision of Henry's principal classical temple, the Pantheon (1753), sitting broad and bright on a grassy bank above the water, framed by trees. It was designed by the architect Henry Flitcroft, whom Henry used for most of his garden buildings. It consists of a wide low dome, in the manner of the 113–125AD Roman Pantheon, fronted by a large portico and pediment. The whole edifice is wide and broad, so that it sits substantially and comfortably on its mound. This is no pepper-pot or shoe-box temple: it has effortless dignity.

LEFT The Pantheon, broadly based on the Pantheon in Rome, was built upon a formal turf mound which, at various stages in its history, has been covered by a looser, more romantic layer of shrubs. Whether these were planted or self-sown is not known.

RIGHT The portico of the Pantheon leads through a massive door to the inner chamber, and its gallery of towering statues.

## A Place Fit for the Gods

Henry took his path from the Grotto to the Pantheon obliquely, so that one emerges from the trees not to face the Pantheon's façade square-on, but sideways and close to it, forcing one to look at the view from it – the same wide vista across the water to that same classical and Gothic trio. Only now may one turn and step inside.

The Pantheon had minimal heating so it could be used for entertaining (temples were ever chilly, even in summer) and a circle of statues of gods and goddesses stand high against its walls: a massive Hercules by Rysbrack, holding court over the god Dionysus, the goddesses Venus, Diana, Flora and Isis, St Suzanna and the Greek mythological hero Meleager. Livia Augusta, wife of the first Roman emperor, also appears depicted as Ceres, goddess of agriculture and fertility, which no doubt had resonance for the owner of a large agricultural estate. Light comes from a central skylight as in the Pantheon in Rome, on to a beautifully paved floor. Nothing more. It is a place to pause and consider what these figures represent.

ABOVE *Interior of the Pantheon, Stourhead* by Samuel Woodforde, c.1784, gives a sense of the building's contemplative interior.

RIGHT Michael Rysbrack's *Hercules*, a symbol of strength in adversity, was commissioned in 1747, even before the Pantheon was begun.

Henry's path now began its return journey by crossing a rustic bridge with outward views to the landscape beyond the garden proper, to carefully wooded hills and the lake, apparently spreading still further. Now the path crosses the dam itself. At this point one could see both sets of buildings facing each other across the lake, the Pantheon and Grotto on one side, the church and Temple of Flora on the other. To see the view now, populated by visitors on a busy day, is to realise how much fun the garden was, how much it was an architectural *capriccio* intended to raise a smile, a playground for styles and ideas.

But before reaching the church and returning to the mansion there were other amusements. Henry made a

wild and noisy cascade in the valley side, with help from his friend and painter Copplestone Warre Bampfylde, who had made his own cascade-riven landscape garden at Hestercombe in Somerset during the years 1750–80. Henry commissioned Bampfylde to catalogue the grounds at Stourhead and his sketches are some of the most telling images of the garden at that time.

ABOVE The Pantheon (above left) and the view from the Pantheon (above right): the Temple of Flora, Bristol Cross, Stourton Church and Palladian Bridge. Colt Hoare removed some village houses to dignify the view. A small number of cottages remain to the left of the church (they include holiday lets) but are hidden by trees.

LEFT  A Vestal Virgin at the Temple of Apollo.

RIGHT  From the Temple of Apollo: the Pantheon (left), and Grotto (centre). Island trees hide the upper arm of the lake where the high-arched white bridge once crossed the water. In the original conception, there was no visible foreground, no Romantic trees below, but only turf dropping invisibly away.

## A Collection of Cultures

Having invisibly crossed the country road leading to the village by means of a monumental rock arch, Henry now offered a choice: either to see his Hermitage made of tree stumps with bones scattered inside and a candle always burning (he quite fancied being the hermit himself – 'I believe I shall put myself in to be the hermit,' he remarked to his daughter) or to mount the steep wooded hillside and emerge on a grassy plateau where stood his Temple of Apollo, or Sun Temple.

This ornate drum-shaped building was based on the ancient Roman Temple of Venus at Baalbek in Lebanon, then well known from Robert Wood's *The Ruins of Balbec*, published in 1757. From here, there was the view of the entire garden – temples, grotto, church, village, and in the distance that perilous arching bridge where the journey began.

RIGHT The highly ornate Temple of Apollo once held statues in each of its niches. During one of its twentieth-century refurbishments the dome was resurfaced with a Ruberoid compound.

RIGHT  Seen from the Temple of Flora, the Temple of Apollo looks out through its opening in the trees. It is the only temple to stand high above the water with the ability to command views of the entire garden.

FAR RIGHT  The Temple of Flora, framed by young trees. In the very earliest stages of the garden, it had its own small formal water garden with statuary.

It only remained to descend to the village, this time through a rocky tunnel under the road, and to inspect the Gothic Greenhouse, Chinese Umbrella and Temple of Flora inscribed with words in Latin, again from the *Aeneid*. They are a warning, as Aeneas seeks to enter the Underworld: 'Keep away, oh, keep far away you who are profane!' The path leads finally up through the woodland to the house once more, leaving Henry's idyllic landscape behind and below.

If a Chinese Umbrella sounds a step too far even for Henry's catholic architectural tastes, one should remember that this was a garden following contemporary preoccupations, and in the 1740s and '50s things Chinese were thoroughly in fashion. Stowe, yet again, toyed with the Chinese, as did Studley Royal. Chiswick House had a go at Egyptian. Henry even made a Turkish Tent painted blue and white to resemble tiles, in the manner of Hamilton's tent at Painshill. Stourhead showed the known world in one picture, ordered and understood.

## The Greatest Vista

It is at the village that the greatest of Stourhead's set-piece views was to be found, a vista looking past the Bristol High Cross and over the Palladian Bridge to the Pantheon across the water on its grassy mound. Henry proudly described it to his daughter in 1762 as 'a charming Gasp'd picture', referring to his beloved Gaspard Dughet. Certainly at that time there was a strong school of thought that said composing a garden was like composing a picture – a Claude, a Poussin or a Gaspard Dughet. The poet Alexander Pope declared that 'All gardening is landscape painting – just like a landscape hung up.'

It has been suggested that in view of the garden's nods to the *Aeneid* it could have been Claude's well-known painting, now in the National Gallery in London, of the *Landscape with Aeneas at Delos* (1672) that directly inspired this great set-piece view from the church to the Pantheon. There are similarities, certainly – the great domed temple, the bridge, water – but nothing was ever spoken or written about it, which, if it were true, seems odd.

There by the church, Henry developed the Spread Eagle Inn, from where tourists could visit the landscape garden, although they would be starting, as it were, from its wrong end. Visiting gardens such as Stourhead was popular amongst the well-to-do and owners would often build an inn for visitors, where they could stay and pay for a tour with the head gardener. Stowe had an inn by 1717. Sometimes there was a guidebook (Lord Cobham had one, as did Henry's successor at Stourhead).

But here is a curious thing. That greatest view of the garden could be seen from the main road through the village, even though it was the culmination of Henry's sequestered garden. A traveller would drive down into the village past lodges and gatehouse, and straight ahead through the trees, see the 10.7m (35ft) Bristol High Cross, an ancient Gothic cross (like a church spire) that had stood at a crossroads in the centre of Bristol since 1373, and which was rescued by Henry and re-erected here. Today it is wholly bare stone, but in Henry's day the figurines on its sides were painted blue, red and gold. That traveller, drawn on by the intriguing spectacle of the Cross, would have instantly been presented with that glorious view across the water to the Pantheon. The opportunity for public gaze can only have been intentional, an image Henry was pleased to share with the world.

ABOVE The Spread Eagle Inn was developed by Henry and his successor Richard Colt Hoare to accommodate visitors to the garden. It is still busy today. The eagle can be found in the Hoare family crest, as seen in the vases which now stand beside the main door of the mansion (see pages 16–17).

LEFT The Bristol Cross, once colourfully painted, was an eye-catcher for anyone first entering the village by road. It marks a public viewpoint for that great view across the water to the Pantheon.

## The Vision of the Painter-Gardener

Henry would not have recognised the dazzling gardens of the late nineteenth or twentieth centuries, so biased as they were towards colour, when his own greatest pleasure was in varied greens and light and shade and architecture. We are used to botanical complexity even in gardens on the scale of Stourhead. We expect them to have great plant collections; we think of that as normal. And so it is important today to remember, when looking at Stourhead, that Henry's garden has had 200 years of romantic, plantsman's gardening laid upon it. Henry's green open spaces on the shores and around buildings have been reduced in size by glorious plantings of new and dramatic trees and shrubs. Henry's islands are now home to tall trees which close off vistas across the lake. It is beautiful and satisfying, but very different.

Consider Bampfylde's 1775 images of the garden. There you see the Pantheon freer of trees and the Temple of Apollo standing on a far barer hillside, the dam a clean arc of turf, so that the cultural and literary ideas to which those buildings allude are loud and clear. Nature was closely managed, just as a painter might arrange it, but very definitely not allowed to seem in charge. Granted the planting is immature in Bampfylde's images, but still, Henry's was a cleaner, crisper, greener, more open garden than we see today. It pushed its ideas clearly forward; the planting was there not to soften or envelop them but to frame them.

# Last Days

What were Henry's plans for Stourhead after his death? As a penultimate tragedy, his son and heir, Henry, died of smallpox in Naples aged 21, just as Henry was about to build the Pantheon. His last daughter died in 1783, leaving him altogether childless. He named as his heir his newly married grandson Richard Colt Hoare, to whom he then handed over Stourhead. Henry retired to a brick villa in Clapham, the Wilderness, which Flitcroft had built for him 30 years before, and he died two years later, aged 80.

Henry's achievement was to have made the bones of the garden at Stourhead, a skeleton which future generations might clothe and alter according to their tastes. It was admired at the time by almost everyone. The professional designer, Capability Brown, came to occupy gardening's centre stage after 1750, and another diary entry made by Mrs Philip Lybbe Powys said of Stourhead that, 'Brown could not have executed it with more grace and elegance.' In 1762 Horace Walpole, bitchiest of garden pundits, in his *Visits to Country Seats*, admired the view from the Temple of Apollo, the lake full of swans and tame carp, and declared it 'one of the most picturesque scenes in the world'.

LEFT Bampfylde's 1775 view shows Henry's garden freer of trees, the Temple of Apollo standing free on its grassy open hillside, and the scene animated by animals, birds and roads, boats and carriages; it is an outward-looking and altogether more living landscape. Subsequently it was made more inward-looking and horticulturally focused, a cat's cradle of intersecting vistas within a colourful woodland bowl.

LEFT Since the nineteenth century the Temple of Apollo has stood within the trees, rather than on Henry's original open hillside (see Bampfylde's illustration on the previous page).

# The Genius of Stourhead

That Stourhead is a special place is without question; its individual elements merge together to create a magical work of art. The most remarkable thing about the garden is that it has survived with no physical destruction or major loss of content, although elements were almost lost in the 1930s. Importantly, it has survived all the changes in and threats from 'tastes' in gardening that have taken place from its conception in the 1740s to its transfer of care and ownership from the Hoare family to the National Trust in 1946.

Stourhead is far more than a garden simply laid out on paper by an owner and designer; there is a real story and personality, deep intelligence and careful consideration behind every decision that was made as Henry the Magnificent created his piece of heaven on earth with help from architect Henry Flitcroft. The garden is more than a collection of pleasantly placed architectural features, carefully chosen trees and shrubs and a great lake that was making a statement about status in society. Through the architecture we can trace personal journeys across Europe and literary interests; we can plot the seasons and the corners of the world in the plant collection

RIGHT Henry Hoare II really did care for the surroundings and kept his grand interventions to their simplest form where necessary. This consideration helped create the perfect relationship between the contemporary and the traditional.

and see the interest that the Hoares took in the plants of the time; the lake tells of considered design – not too big and not too small, perfectly judged for the estate and how it sits within the landscape. Hoare really consulted the 'Genius of the Place'.

The Conservation Plan for Stourhead was one of the first ever to be drawn up for a garden in England back in the 1970s. At the time, it was becoming increasingly important to the National Trust and for Stourhead that the garden had a restoration plan and an appropriate direction in which to move. The National Trust had been caring for Stourhead since 1946 and the majority of the work, up until the 1970s, had been repairs to structures and basic maintenance across the estate. The forestry team had mostly overseen the garden, as the trees needed much thinning and many dangerous specimens had to be removed. The long-term vision never really made it onto the list. But a garden of nearly 300 years' maturity needed a plan, it needed to be considered beyond the next week, months or the course of a few years – it should have a planned journey ahead of it. The future layout, design, plant collection and spirit of the place was in the hands of the National Trust and those of the great minds of the organisation at the time, and they wanted to get it right. It needed to be ground-breaking to honour the magnificent history of the place. Conversations began in 1973 and it was 1978

LEFT The planting at Stourhead has inevitably evolved, but the original intentions of its designers are always kept in mind.

before the conservation plan was published; much of it is still relevant today.

Every Head Gardener is different. We all have our own personal likes and dislikes and we approach work in our own way, but the garden at Stourhead is a constant. There have been five permanent Head Gardeners at Stourhead, including myself, since the 1950s. I know three of them well and we are all very different people. The conservation plan was designed to ensure that Stourhead was respected and that the garden was carefully restored in a manner appropriate to its history, avoiding the interference and influence of individuals. It's a simple and concise document that covers 64 pages and includes a brief historical context and developments; the garden itself is set out in management areas with associated precedents and proposals to match; there is also a brief planting policy for the garden included. I now love working with this and other documents in managing the garden; they are the tools I use to paint and re-create the picture. I am often asked: 'Do you feel restricted by the history of the garden, do you feel your own creativity is being held back?' My answer is always 'Not at all.' I love looking back into the archives, getting to know the details that led to the creation of the garden I know so well; I like to apply my accumulated knowledge to the management of the garden. My professional passions apply to every element of my work on the garden; Garden History, Arboriculture and Horticulture; they are all essential to the understanding and good management of the garden.

Gardening is obviously a personal passion that grew into a professional career. I was lucky to discover my niche early on – a garden steeped in history, fascinating in design, covered in trees and open to the public. All of the work we do as a garden team, all the information I put together to feed into the work schedule that the team then implements, and the approach we take to every element of what we do, are rewarded when we see or hear the reaction of the visitors to the garden, as it was for Henry the Magnificent.

It's the details that make the difference to the overall impression. The formative work on the tree collection, for example, can have a huge impact on the visual style seen in the garden. We assess the position and shape of a tree in a particular area, then analyse the desired style of presentation for that area, marrying both and manipulating the tree to enhance the style; it is simply magical to be able to contribute to this process. Every little adjustment helps to paint the living picture within the garden. Many of the clues to the various styles of presentation around the estate can come from the conservation plan contents, but I also like to look at paintings and drawings of eighteenth-century period gardens and try to see in them what their owners would see, and then try to replicate that for the visitors to the garden today.

My interests have gone far beyond the trees, shrubs and plants, beyond the beauty of the place, and have merged into an overall appreciation of the true genius that has gone into the planning and care of this magnificent paradise over the last 300 years.

# Richard Colt Hoare

## (1758–1838)

# The Next Generation

Richard Colt Hoare would be the third great figure in the making of Stourhead, after Good Henry, the builder, and Henry the Magnificent, the gardener. Colt Hoare was, in fact, both a builder and gardener, but in a quieter, subtler manner.

His early life had been spent in the family house at Barn Elms, Putney, in what is now West London. Holidays were spent at his grandfather's house, Stourhead, where he had a vast garden to explore and could watch the construction of such extraordinary sights as the Temple of Apollo and the arrival and complicated reassembly of the Bristol Cross. In middle age he looked back on his time at Stourhead and admitted it had given him 'a love for the beauties of both Nature and Art'. But it must have been exciting, as well as educational. What did he make of it as a 14-year-old when Alfred's Tower was completed and he could climb those gloomy stairs and gaze on the wide views from 49m (160ft) in the air?

He turned into a studious young man and suitable material for taking on the responsibility of the house and garden; Henry gave him an allowance of £2,000 a year at 21 and a house in Lincoln's Inn Fields. But Henry had still bigger plans. He wanted Stourhead to be more secure financially, since, for all the great income the bank could bring in, Stourhead was still at risk if the bank, and therefore its owners, should suffer financial collapse. Business was business, but a great estate such as he had created should be timeless, and so he devised a radical means of securing Stourhead's future. He would separate permanently and completely the house and the bank by handing Stourhead to Colt Hoare on condition that he relinquish his part in the bank. He must go his own way as a wealthy landowner; the bank must take care of itself, for richer, for poorer, in the capable hands of his brother's branch of the family. The plan did not go down well at the bank, but it happened nonetheless.

To Henry's equally great satisfaction he managed, in 1783, to engineer Colt Hoare's marriage to Hester Lyttelton of Hagley Hall, near Birmingham, where, through the 1740s and '50s, a large and remarkable landscape garden had been made.

With these objectives in place, Henry retired to Clapham and Colt Hoare, together with his new bride, came to Stourhead. His mission was accomplished. And to complete the picture Hester gave birth to a son. A Henry, of course.

Or perhaps it was not quite accomplished. The elderly Henry died a couple of years later, but Hester died in childbirth the same year. To Colt Hoare, newly installed at Stourhead, it must have smacked of Henry's tragic life all over again and that was enough for him. Within weeks he set off for the fresh air of the Continent to fill his mind with art and antiquity, leaving behind his little son for six whole years.

However studious he was by nature, Colt Hoare was brave too, for in those days long-distance travel was no pleasure, even if one took a fellow companion as he did – Captain Meyrick, a family friend of his wife Hester. Crossing the dangerous English Channel in a boat could

PREVIOUS PAGE The Pantheon
and to its right the Grotto, close by
the water. Note again the contrast
of light and shade.

RIGHT Sir Richard Colt Hoare
(1758–1838) with his son Henry,
who died two years before he
could take over Stourhead from
his father. Painted by Samuel
Woodforde, 1795.

take three days. Six days later he was in Paris, after which he crossed the Alps by mule, in chairs slung between poles, and descended through Turin and Florence to Rome, the goal of all Grand Tourists. At their next stop, Naples, Meyrick died of malaria contracted in the Pontine Marshes south of Rome, a region notorious for disease (they would only finally be made safe by Mussolini's large drainage programmes in the 1930s). In 22 months, Colt Hoare travelled 10.864km (6,751 miles).

At home, his father was knighted but died shortly afterwards in 1787, leaving Colt Hoare now a Baronet himself and with another grand house in St James's Square. He came home briefly but was soon back in Europe, feeding his academic soul while managing his estate at arm's length. This time he went eastwards, to Holland, Brussels, Potsdam, Prague, Hungary, Vienna, Trieste and Venice. Thereafter he returned to familiar ground, down through Florence and Siena to Rome, buying pictures as had Henry before him, and finally reaching that great treasure house of ancient ruins, Sicily, where his many sketches would make material for his 1819 book, *A Classical Tour Through Italy and Sicily*. Only in 1791 did he finally come home to England.

# Academic Interests

It might have been expected that Colt Hoare would remarry on his return to England, but he did not. Instead, like his uncle, he settled down to the serious business of developing Stourhead, secure in the knowledge that he too had a son, Henry, to take over in due course, as well as various London houses, 4,452ha (11,000 acres) and a baronetcy.

During his time in Europe he had amassed a large collection of paintings, sculpture and books which, as a passionate antiquarian, he wanted around him and well enough displayed for them to be a constant pleasure and something he could share with others (barely home a year, he had already become a Fellow of the Royal Society and of the Society of Dilettanti. Fellowship of the Society of Antiquaries of London followed). His collection would soon include works by such greats as Gainsborough, Titian, Canaletto, Rubens and Leonardo da Vinci. Plainly the house at Stourhead, as his grandfather had left it, was not large enough for his purposes and he set about expanding it (see page 90).

He began to give the British landscape the same kind of academic and artistic study he had given to Italy's, spending much of the next two decades travelling through the wilder parts of Britain to look at its history, archaeology and topography, on roads that were just as hazardous as those of the Alps, if not more so. Wales, as noted by other travellers, had the worst roads of all. To get to southern Wales in the days before the modern Severn Bridge was constructed (as recently as 1966), it was necessary to make a great northward loop via Gloucester to cross the river, or to brave a dangerous ferry over the estuary which, in Colt Hoare's time, could take anywhere between 15 minutes and 2½ hours.

Colt Hoare loved Wales, even buying himself a fishing lodge at Bala in the historic northern county of Merioneth (now Gwynedd) in 1796. That same year he got as far as the west coast and saw Thomas Johnes' (pronounced 'Jones') great landscape garden at Hafod, near Aberystwyth, noting its excellent inn built at the Devil's Bridge for garden visitors, like his own Spread Eagle Inn. It was the mountainous landscape of Wales and its ruined abbeys that appealed to him, as they did to that other famous traveller and writer William Gilpin, who was later to see Stourhead and be only moderately impressed when he mentioned it in his *Observations on the Western Parts of England* (1798). But by 1804 Colt Hoare was able to publish his own account of his Welsh trips and in 1807 of his Irish ones. His library of topographical books grew.

So earnest was Colt Hoare about the importance of local history that he had bought Glastonbury Tor in 1876, while he was first in Italy, no doubt inspired by childhood images of it rising from the mist as he stood at the top of Alfred's Tower. In 1804 he restored the tower on top of the Tor, which remains a familiar Somerset landmark. He was fascinated by Stonehenge and the many barrows that dotted the Wiltshire landscape, opening some barrows for the first time himself to archaeological investigation. It led to him writing *The History of Ancient Wiltshire*, published in parts. *The History*

*of Modern Wiltshire*, followed, to cover more recent places of importance, including his own Stourhead.

Colt Hoare developed an interest in botany, which led to him being elected a Fellow of the Linnaean Society (1812). It was a time when the introduction of new plants from abroad was rapidly expanding. So much was new that gardens and academic botany became thoroughly intertwined, and as if to underline this flurry of interest a Horticultural Society (now the Royal Horticultural Society) was formed in 1804. Men of wealth were able to develop private collections in the name of science and beauty, such as the collection of pelargoniums brought together at Croome Park, Worcestershire, by Lord Coventry who also made a landscape garden with Capability Brown. It was Brown's first great commission, and Brown, too, was a customer of Hoare's bank. By the 1790s there were 103 kinds of pelargonium at Croome, some of them named to honour Coventry's endeavours, and the collection was rapidly expanding. Similarly at Stourhead, under glass in a conservatory attached to the corner of the house (1814), Colt Hoare began to develop a collection of pelargoniums brought back from Africa, starting with 53 in 1809 and amassing over 600 different species and varieties by 1821. One subdivision of the genus *Pelargonium* was named *Hoarea* in his honour.

ABOVE Colt Hoare, a fellow of the Linnaean Society, developed a collection of over 600 species and varieties of pelargonium, many of which are still grown at Stourhead today.

RIGHT The glasshouse in the Walled Garden is home to a re-established collection of pelargonium.

# Extending the House

It is no surprise that with so much to display and so many books to house, Colt Hoare enlarged his grandfather's house. It was then still the foursquare Palladian villa, liveable, but without space to display his collections adequately. Before her untimely death his wife, Hester, had described the house as 'modern' and stylistically the villa was certainly up to date. But other things failed to please: she found 'frightful' the room with pillars whose capitals were shaped like palm trees (probably Egyptian-style), and said, 'the upper part of the house is very bad. The rooms being few and sadly furnished.'

Colt Hoare spent ten years making his alterations to Stourhead, the most significant of which were two large pavilions of his own design, largely complete by 1805, in which year he was appointed High Sheriff of Wiltshire, recognition indeed of his established place in landed society. The pavilions were set either side of the main block of the existing house but linked to it, made in keeping with the style of architecture, and well-suited to the Palladian central block. Both wings, apart from their basements, contained only one large room, each dedicated to its academic purpose.

One wing was to be his library where his books created a scholarly sanctum. It was an important collection, especially of the history of South West England, and in 1825 his Italian historical and topographical works were gratefully received by the British Museum. Thomas Chippendale the Younger was employed to make fine library chairs, monumentally

large desks, and steps to reach the upper shelves; indeed the generous volume of work created at Stourhead saved Chippendale from bankruptcy in 1804 and he continued to work for Colt Hoare for many years after that. Colt Hoare also recommended him to Charles Hoare for his house at Luscombe, where Brown's successor Humphry Repton was making the garden.

Covering the library floor was an Axminster carpet specially woven to resemble the pattern of tiled Roman pavement, and at the far end of the barrel-vaulted

ABOVE  Colt Hoare's library wing of 1805, furnished by Thomas Chippendale the Younger, with an arched glass painting by Francis Egginton. The carpet imitates Roman tiling. The original paintings were sold in the nineteenth century and windows inserted on the right.

LEFT  Library steps by Chippendale. Colt Hoare was a loyal patron of this brilliant craftsman and designer and his work at Stourhead saw Chippendale through financial difficulties.

ceiling was a semi-circular window of painted glass by Francis Egginton, stretching the whole width of the room, showing Apollo and the Muses in Parnassus. At the opposite end of the room above the bookshelves was a sister painting the same size and shape by Samuel Woodforde, of *Parnassus, flanked by the figures of Strength and Temperance*, copied from work by Raphael in the Vatican. It was Woodforde who painted the huge portrait of Colt Hoare and his son that now stands in the Entrance Hall with the rest of the family portraits (see page 85).

LEFT Colt Hoare's gallery wing, furnished by Chippendale, built to house the family's pictures properly. Windows, set on the east side only, could be shuttered to exclude light and preserve the colours.

RIGHT *The Adoration of the Magi*, by Ludovico Cardi (Cigoli), 1605 (shown left) from Henry the Magnificent's collection and *Marchese Niccolò Maria Pallavicini guided to the Temple of Vertù by Apollo, with a Self-Portrait of the Artist*, by Carlo Maratta, 1705 (shown right), from Colt Hoare's collection.

The other new wing was to be a picture gallery, something more for the wider world than his library and which therefore was given its own access to the outside for visitors. It had windows on the east side only and could be blacked out when not in use to preserve the paintings. Pride of place went to three massive canvases: the *Adoration of the Magi*, by Cigoli (1559–1613) which he had bought himself and for which Chippendale made a magnificent frame; Henry's *Marchese Niccolò Maria Pallavicini guided to the Temple of Virtù by Apollo*, by Carlo Maratta (1625–1713) and a companion piece commissioned by Henry in 1759 from Anton Raphael Mengs, of *Octavian and Cleopatra*. Contemporary paintings included a pair of melodramatic portraits, *Distress by Land* and *Distress by Sea*, both by Henry Thomson (1773–1843).

Like Woodforde, the artist J.M.W. Turner was promoted by Colt Hoare; Turner visited Stourhead in 1799, producing a painting titled *Lake Avernus: Aeneas and the Cumaean Sibyl* based on a sketch made in Italy by Colt Hoare himself. It hung at Stourhead until it was sold in

1883. Commissions from Turner included a fine set of architectural drawings of Salisbury Cathedral, hung in the Library.

Colt Hoare found great excitement in the work of the Swiss artist Louis Ducros (1748–1810), whose watercolours, he said, like Turner's, seemed to have elevated the medium far beyond its previous capabilities. Watercolours, said Colt Hoare, were not of the same 'higher class of painting as oils but Turner's architectural drawings of Salisbury [cathedral] will never be surpassed'. But by 1822 Colt Hoare wrote of Ducros: 'To him I attribute the first knowledge and power of water-colours.' He had 11 large drawings by Ducros at Stourhead, protected from the light and unfaded after 30 years.

It was another of his favoured painters, Francis Nicholson (1753–1844), who Colt Hoare commissioned to make paintings of the garden in 1813 (see page 100), just as Bampfylde had recorded Henry's garden in 1775 (see pages 72–73).

# *Alterations to the Garden*

While Colt Hoare's work on the house was mainly in the form of additions, his work on the garden was to a large extent a taking away of features and a restyling of what remained through different planting. In the broadest sense he created the garden as we know it today. Nor was his work on the garden a collaboration as Henry's had been; he had no Flitcroft to work with as architect, no Bampfylde with whom to build a cascade and discuss his ideas. And yet his work was very much of its time.

On his Welsh trips he had seen the gardens of Richard Payne Knight at Downton Castle and Uvedale Price at Foxley, whose ideas would be so stylistically and publicly at war with those of Capability Brown's natural successor, Humphry Repton. The two Herefordshire squires favoured a wilder, more picturesque landscape garden over Repton's more comfortable and domesticated manner.

Colt Hoare was aware of the increasing desire for gardens to be much wilder than those of the early eighteenth century, where formality on a landscape scale had played a large part, and in which the clean lines and open spaces of his grandfather Henry's garden had been rooted. Colt Hoare's garden would be softer, more naturalistic, and richer in its planting materials – more romantic, more 'Wordsworthian', if not actually wilder.

## The Changing Face of Stourhead

One of the significant, and most invisible, of Colt Hoare's alterations to the garden must be the removal of the steps that led down into it from the house. In Campbell's original house a pair of central stairs on the south side led down from the piano nobile and across the lawn to where the statue of Apollo offered the choice of the Terrace walk or descent into the Virgilian landscape. But as Colt Hoare's library wing had effectively left the stairs no longer in the centre of the façade (which their grandeur plainly demanded), he removed them altogether.

Colt Hoare's greatest visible alteration around the house was the dismantling and reconstruction of Henry's grand Clock Arch gatehouse to a new position at the entrance to the drive, marking one's arrival in the Stourhead domain and leading up to the front door on the east side, where the full extent of his new wings could be fully appreciated. It was from this door that one now entered the garden. From here, too, it was possible

to place in that wonderful rolling Wiltshire landscape two great houses rising in the distance: Fonthill Abbey and New Wardour Castle. Meanwhile, in the village, Gothic details were added to the inn and church, cottages were removed to improve the view of the church from across the lake and the public road was separated from the garden by a fence.

Among Colt Hoare's first moves in the landscape garden proper was the removal of many of Henry's smaller architectural garden features – the Chinese Umbrella, the Turkish Tent, the Gothic Greenhouse, the Venetian Seat and more. To his mind, trained in rigorous classicism, they were an intrusion upon good taste and detracted from fine buildings like the Pantheon. (Would he have also removed Alfred's Tower if it had been made as first intended, as St Mark's Tower, Venice?) These excised features took with them a certain amount of what had made the garden fun; under Colt Hoare the garden would be both more serious and more romantic. No surprise, then, that Henry's amusing Hermitage was scrapped in the same year (1814) in which a conservatory for botanical purposes was erected by the house. Of course, garden buildings decay just like houses (the history of the Grotto and Temple of Apollo had been one of endless repair ever since their construction) and there are always decisions to be made about whether to keep pouring money into something that is decaying but was created mostly for fun. Colt Hoare is not to be blamed for taking a pragmatic attitude to the question of expense at odds with his own preferences. Gardens change over time.

## The Triumph of Pragmatism

Most significant of his removals was the 'frightful' white wooden Palladian bridge that arched over the top arm of the lake connecting the house to the Grotto and Pantheon. It was collapsing. In Colt Hoare's own guidebook to the garden of 1800, he states that: 'A Ferry-boat now supplies the place of a Palladian, or Chinese Bridge, which, in its architecture, ill accorded with the different Grecian buildings around it.' Certainly there was a flavour of the Chinese about it. Perhaps Colt Hoare was looking for an excuse to take it away; he was far more comfortable with European architecture, whatever its origin and the antiquarian classicist in him proposed that 'the most interesting building which adorns these gardens is an ancient Gothic Cross, perhaps the richest and best preserved of any now existing in England.'

Did the loss of the bridge matter? Yes and no. It meant that the garden's circuit path now had to divert north around the head of the lake to get to the Grotto. More importantly, when viewed from the bottom end of the lake, its absence removed that satisfying sense of a circuit, of seeing where one had been and where one had come from, the pleasure of recognition, and, of course, the fun of crossing the 'frightful' thing in the first place. Now the water in that upper arm of the lake just disappeared into the trees and the late nineteenth-century tulip tree planted on one of the islands finished the job by hiding the head of the lake altogether.

At the same time, Colt Hoare made some architectural additions to the garden, but for practical reasons to do with how the garden was used. A boathouse was built on the lakeshore near the Temple of Flora, a rocky construction echoing the Grotto opposite. A small garden service building between the Grotto and the Pantheon was given a pretty Gothic makeover, with a little porch, pointed windows, a roof of thatch, and a stone seat from which to gaze at the water. Perhaps this Gothic Cottage was another picnic spot. Alfred's Tower, once not much more than a viewing platform, was given a less frightful room at the top, from which to gaze towards Glastonbury in a little more comfort.

LEFT  Colt Hoare's rustic boathouse will have provided a pleasurable route across the lake when the wooden Palladian bridge had been removed.

RIGHT  The Gothic Cottage, once a garden service building, was given an pretty and practical makeover.

## Planting on a Grand Scale

Paths which has once been grass were replaced with gravel, which, of course, was far more comfortable underfoot and easier-going when the ground was wet, but it also formalised the way the garden was to be explored, gave an instruction rather than a suggestion of where to go. It began to remove the sense of walking *in* the landscape and to replace it with a walk *through* the landscape, looking at something from the comfort of a gravel path rather than being wholly a part of it.

In his day, Henry had not been averse to planting amongst his native trees the odd exotic species, such as the cedar of Lebanon and Norway spruce, but by and large he stuck to those which were part of the traditional English landscape. Colt Hoare now used a broader brush, adding more exotic trees from other continents and bringing more changes in colour and texture to the treescape which defined the garden. In came pink horse-chestnuts, false acacias, tulip trees, sweet gums, swamp cypresses and even variegated sycamores. Up on the Terrace, the Fir Walk was felled, perhaps because its craggy heads were sticking out gracelessly from the woodland canopy, but their removal is indicative of the general replacement of any kind of formality, straight or curved, with a softening of more trees.

It was Colt Hoare who seriously began the planting of shrubs at Stourhead, and, once again it changed the perspective of the garden. Instead of the point of the garden being long vistas through greenery to architectural eyecatchers in the distance, the flowering foreground became something as valued as the long view. Rhododendrons of various species began to arrive in large numbers, especially the mauve-purple *Rhododendron ponticum*, attractive enough in itself and *en masse* but invasive, and cherry laurel (*Prunus laurocerasus*). The change must have been more dramatic than we can realise today, for English woodlands do not have heavy, broad-leaved evergreens other than holly that could so solidly close in an airy woodland. In the 1800s the change must have been shocking. Woods that in winter had been open-textured and offered filtered views would now be dense with all-year foliage; yes, the new evergreens would intensify that contrast between light and shade that Henry so enjoyed, but they would also bring a dark brush to bear on a brighter picture. It was the gloom of the Romantic period, and a controlling gloom at that, very firm about where it allowed you to look or not look.

LEFT Colt Hoare introduced large quantities of the purple *Rhododendron ponticum*, while later generations added more brightly coloured hybrids.

Colt Hoare was a great planter of laurel in general, creating 'laurel lawns' under mature trees, flat-topped understoreys less than 1m (3ft 3in) tall, which offered a green forest floor rather than brown leaf litter. Laurel has a wonderful ability to reflect light from its shiny leaves and would have brought illumination to mature woodland.

But he did yet more with laurels. He planted up areas which in Henry's garden had been open space, most noticeably the grassy hillside upon which the Temple of Apollo stood. It reinforced again the way in which the buildings now emerged from a mysterious covering of vegetation, rather than being presented for the viewer's contemplation in their open empty spaces. It was a different way of looking at things. Henry's more spacious treatment is clearly visible in Bampfylde's illustrations of 1770 and is still there in S.H. Grimm's view of 1790, made while Colt Hoare was still away in Italy and before any changes had yet been made by him. But by the time of Nicholson's images from 1813, when Colt Hoare had been planting for 20 years, things were very different.

Barratt and Son's *Description of Stourhead*, of 1818, notes that ivy, that most romantic of climbers, growing on the Temple of Apollo, 'may prove detrimental to the fabric, yet in a picturesque point of view, we cannot desire its absence.' Was this Colt Hoare experimenting with the idea of the 'romantic ruin'? Nicholson's illustration of 1813 clearly shows ivy there, as well as some very romantic and craggy bare rock. Colt Hoare

had visited the ruined priory at Llanthony in Wales in 1793, 1798 and 1803, noting its gradual collapse, and said 'I approve of ivy when it hides deformities, not when it conceals beauties.'

Colt Hoare was certainly serious about the condition of his estate in general, and conscientiously repaired houses and built lodges and cottages. He thinned recent plantations just as carefully as he planted new ones, sometimes by the process of merely scattering acorns.

Colt Hoare died at the age of 80, by which time his son Henry ought to have been fit to take over. Sadly it was not so. Henry, it turned out, was less than responsible in his life and duties. He did marry, but only produced a daughter, and meanwhile he ran up embarrassing debts that had to be settled by his father. He died at 52, two years before Colt Hoare himself, whose days ended rheumatic, deaf and pained by gout, busily completing his works on Wiltshire history.

ABOVE The last 150 years have added many darker shades of foliage to the garden.

LEFT Francis Nicholson's illustration of 1813. Warm evening light slants across one of Colt Hoare's gravel paths at the Temple of Flora.

# The Trees of Stourhead

A plant collection can be viewed in quite a sterile way as a simple and diverse living list of plants. However, once you start to consider the individuals within the collection, the whole thing takes on a new and deeper dimension. Each plant will have a story associated with the place, one of the owners or a particular passion that characterised the time. Quite often a plant will have a connection to a brave and committed plant hunter who travelled the world in search of new and exotic species to bring home. As the gardener and custodian of these plants, you begin to learn about the dates they were first introduced into this country from their place of origin, when they were first planted in the garden, and which member of the family was sufficiently taken with this plant to add it to the collection. My role includes all of this and more. I see those trees and shrubs begin to fade through the latter years of their lives, develop structural issues, fungal infections and succumb to the forces that Mother Nature throws at them: it can be emotional. On the flipside, I put spade to soil and prepare the ground to accept new trees or shrubs into the garden; I witness success in the collection as buds break and branches

RIGHT The trees are the ever-changing picture frame in the garden. The appropriate level of care is critical to ensure their survival and eventual replacement.

RIGHT Having the ability to climb the trees allows us as a team to prune them correctly, and also to enhance the historic views framed by the trees.

elongate. During my time at Stourhead, I have seen saplings flourish into young trees and take their place proudly in the garden.

After a few weeks on the team, I started tree-climbing as the arborist, and I began to work on the garden; you really get to know a tree once you've climbed it. From a distance, a particular tree will have a unique shape, almost like a fingerprint, within the treescape. The outline of the canopy acts like a map, plotting the growth pattern of the tree, the branches and scars on the stem marking the successes and failures throughout the life of the individual specimen. The tree's location within the landscape and subsequent growth form will have a unique relationship with the elements.

Climbing into a tree gives a very different perspective; it becomes personal and involves effort. There is a feeling of respect between climber and majestic tree. I have climbed some very notable and worthy specimens in the garden over the years; some are one of a kind and others planted by the great Henry the Magnificent who created the garden. First I will acknowledge that the tree I am about to climb is a living organism and populated with many more; the work about to be done is to benefit the tree and help it through the next phase of its life – potentially up to 200 years in some cases. As the rope is uncoiled and prepares to be launched over the branches above, a conversation will start in my mind, the wonder begins. I hope the tree will offer a pleasant ascent and respect will be mutual. My eyes will trace the route through the limbs and along the trunk to my eventual anchor point – easy enough in the mind, but not so much for the body. 'No surprises please,' I usually ask, and there have been a few: hornets' nests, squirrel drays, massive fractures, stagnant cavities and failing limbs; none were visible or apparent from the ground or seen during my assessment.

In those early days, tree-climbing was a pleasure, my limbs worked effortlessly as I clambered through the trees, my hands comfortable on the rope. My legs would propel me towards my next supporting point, and my feet would launch me from the trunk outwards toward the midpoint of a branch where I would land cleanly and safely. I could progress to the extremities unhindered as if the safety rope was invisible. Slinging my leg through the fork of a branch at 20m (65½ft) above the ground, I would turn and see the garden laid out for me from this unique and privileged vantage point, I was very lucky indeed on all counts. Today, it's a little different: my limbs are older, my mind is wiser and frustratingly more cautious; the fluent synapses that once linked my brain and body are fading and being replaced by the ability to reforecast the garden's budget, complete a risk assessment, undertake Personal Reviews with the team, contribute to interpretation meetings and deal with complaints. Walking the garden today, I know what it's like to be in the canopy of the trees, I know the kind trees that welcomed me and gave me easy passage into them to work. There are also the *bastard trees*, the ones for which I can remember the mammoth effort it took to conquer them. As Lou, my wife, said to me recently as we walked the garden, it is quicker to ask me about the trees I haven't climbed at Stourhead.

I also remember the shadows – the trees and shrubs we have lost to time, Mother Nature or disease. Meandering through the garden, I can see the population of plants that have faded, the trees that are now stumps and have been recorded in the garden diary for the archivists of the future to discover. The stump I see is a relic of a tree which occupied that space for over 200 years in some cases. Many people will have forgotten its existence and place in the garden, but every time I walk or drive a mower past its spot I can recall its shape, the texture of the trunk, the sadness in seeing its decline and the difficulty in deciding when was best to remove it. Every part of this garden has imprinted a memory on my mind.

RIGHT Every tree has a unique character and the autumnal display shows just how different they all are.

# Three Victorians

## (1838–1894)

PREVIOUS PAGE  From the Temple of Apollo a panorama of almost the whole garden could be seen in Henry's day. Today its prospect is narrower and more channelled by the glorious trees.

LEFT  Colen Campbell's great portico on the east side of the house was finally realised over 100 years after it was planned. That addition completed the façade as we see it today.

RIGHT  Henry's obelisk, or 'Sun Pillar', so named for the golden disc at the top, forms the focus of the view west from the mansion. It was rebuilt by Henry Hugh Hoare during his brief time at Stourhead.

# Sir Henry Hugh Hoare (1762–1841)

Since Colt Hoare's son had predeceased him, Stourhead and the baronetcy went to his cousin Henry Hugh Hoare, who at the age of 76 was only four years younger than Colt Hoare. He was also a partner in the bank, which meant that Henry the Magnificent's desire to keep Stourhead and the bank entirely separate was now confounded.

Henry Hugh cannot have expected to be at Stourhead for long, but happily he had three healthy sons who might take it on after his death. He must also have felt he should do his duty by the ambitions of his illustrious forbears who had created Stourhead because, as soon as he inherited, he set about building Colen Campbell's great portico on the entrance front, which Henry had chosen to omit for the sake of simplicity. With Colt Hoare's two flanking pavilions and now the portico, the house was far grander than its first incarnation. Perhaps as an antiquary himself, if not the scholar that Colt Hoare had been, Henry Hugh felt it was right to complete Campbell's original plan. He also rebuilt in Bath stone the crumbling Obelisk with the gold disk at its top – the Sun Pillar, as Henry Hugh like to call it. Parts of the house were rerooofed, as was the Pantheon.

These endeavours speak well of Henry Hugh because he died only three years after inheriting. And he already had a more modest country house of his own at Wavendon in Buckinghamshire. It had been given a landscape and lake by the designer Richard Woods at the same time as Henry was completing the garden at Stourhead, and Henry Hugh had brought up his children there. No doubt he was attached to it.

# Sir Hugh Richard Hoare (1787–1857)

On Henry Hugh's death in 1841, Stourhead, its 4,452ha (11,000 acres) and the title passed to his eldest son Hugh Richard, then aged 54, who would be in charge of Stourhead for 16 years. Straight away he resigned from the bank, where he was a partner, and moved into Stourhead with his wife Anne.

In the annals of any great family there are always those movers and shakers who create remarkable new things, perhaps a house and a garden, or a bank, which are then admired by generations to come. To them goes the glory. But just as important are those family members who are a safe pair of hands: repairers and improvers who quietly and diligently get on with the job of caring for the estate, without the indulgence of new houses, temples and lakes. Such a man was Hugh Richard. And as he and Anne had no children, his time at Stourhead may be regarded as a quiet but valuable period of consolidation.

In the garden there were ongoing repairs. The rotten footbridge below the Pantheon was replaced, in oak. The Pantheon and Temple of Apollo were repainted. The Temple of Flora was re-roofed, as was the Grotto after the removal of laurels which had grown over and into it – all very picturesque but damaging none-the-less; laurel invasion was a problem that occurred regularly over the life of the garden. As patron of St Peter's Church in Stourton, the building that figures so importantly in the views from the garden and where the garden's makers lie buried, Hugh Richard built a new south aisle.

Until now, the east entrance front of the house had sat directly in the park with no intermediate flower gardening, as was commonly the case in landscape gardens, the principle being that the house was part of the landscape – that the house and its master owned the landscape. Farm animals including deer could graze up

ABOVE  A large altar tomb to the 5th Lord Stourton and his wife (c.1536). The tomb chest is beautifully carved, with canopied niches and blind tracery in Perpendicular style.

RIGHT  St Peter's Church, Stourton, is both part of the old village and part of the garden's architecture. Hugh Richard added the south aisle.

to the house itself. But it was a practice better suited perhaps to the more robust attitudes of the eighteenth century than the polite Victorian era. Hugh Richard now erected an iron park rail to keep the animals back from the entrance steps and the carriage drive.

Across the estate he planted many tens of thousands of trees every year, which sounds a great many, but over the expanse of the grounds it might be regarded as the ongoing maintenance of the woodland economy. It was a sporting estate after all, and woods and timber were important economically; careful annual records were kept of the game shot and the literally thousands of rabbits snared. These totals appeared in the *Stourhead Annals*, a record of each year's significant projects and expenditures, instituted by Colt Hoare when he first arrived and then continued with only one break under his successors.

Hugh Richard was also responsible for introducing some of the largest conifers to be found in the garden today. The later years of his life coincided with the time when the west coast of the USA was being explored and colonised, and the climate, particularly in the North West, turned out to have much in common with the British climate, so many species of tree found their way into commerce here. (A walk in the countryside around Seattle even now will show a whole range of plants that are thoroughly common today in British gardens – trees, shrubs, climbers, perennials and ferns.)

A favourite tree at Stourhead throughout the nineteenth century was the Douglas fir, *Pseudotsuga*

*menziesii*, which comes from the Pacific North West and was introduced in 1827 by David Douglas, the plant collector who famously died in a bear pit. Old Douglas firs are recognisable by their hard, heavily corrugated bark that only develops with age. A few trees have grown to well over 65m (213ft) in Britain, though they can make 100m (328ft) in their natural habitat.

As California was opened up in the mid-nineteenth century, the great redwoods reached Britain: the giant redwood or Wellingtonia, *Sequoiadendron giganteum* in 1853 and in 1843 the coast redwood *Sequoia sempervirens,*

which Hugh Richard planted. Redwoods can live for thousands of years, making them if not the longest-lived trees (that honour goes to a dwarf, desert-dwelling pine) then certainly the biggest living things on earth by volume. Both redwood species are recognisable for their soft, spongy bark which protects them from fire. Their habit in Britain, even when planted in moist, protected valleys like Stourhead's, is to thrive and grow magnificently fast, only to succumb to wind or lightning when their tops extend above the rest of the woodland canopy.

ABOVE The spongey-barked and fire-resistant giant redwood or Wellingtonia was introduced in 1853, when it quickly found its place in the great gardens of Britain, often as avenues.

LEFT The craggy bark of the Douglas fir, *Pseudotsuga menziesii*, becomes more and more deeply fissured as it gets older.

There are some common names which over the centuries have been used to cover a huge range of plants far beyond their technical application. Hundreds of plants that do not belong to the genus *Lilium* have been commonly referred to as lilies because they have vaguely trumpet-shaped flowers: Guernsey lilies, pineapple lilies, calla lilies, foxtail lilies and many more. The name 'fir' has been used similarly, and Good Henry's Fir Walk is quite likely to have comprised Scots pines, *Pinus sylvestris*; true firs belong in the genus *Abies*. There is a similar confusion over cedars: the Western red cedar planted by Hugh Richard, a new import in 1853 from western North America, is botanically nearer to cypress than cedar; it is *Thuja plicata*. Another large forest conifer, it is recognisable partly by the pineapple-like fragrance of its sap and partly by the way the lowest branches of very old specimens lean down to the ground and rise up again, just as they do at Stourhead. The wood is wonderfully light, straight-grained and easy to split, hence its use as roofing shingles. A log which has been cut for a year or more will still give off a delicious fragrance when split.

Sadly, Hugh Richard had no children and so, on his death in 1857, his well-managed estate and the title passed to his nephew, Henry Ainslie Hoare.

LEFT Following the introduction to Stourhead by Colt Hoare of the common purple *Rhododendron ponticum*, brightly coloured hybrids followed well into the twentieth century. They are the antithesis of Good Henry's first all-green garden.

# Sir Henry Ainslie Hoare (1824–94)

If every family has its safe pairs of hands, it also has its black sheep, and Henry Ainslie was certainly better at spending money than making it. But if the master was off enjoying himself at the races or chasing a fox, well, a good agent would see to it that the estate was kept in decent condition on his behalf.

It was understood that Henry Ainslie was less than reliable long before he inherited. He had married Augusta Clayton East the day after he came of age in 1845 and they took their honeymoon at Stourhead rather than travelling. Their daughter Augusta – Gussy – was born very shortly afterwards and a son Charles a more respectable year later. London was their home. He was made a clerk at the bank, yet still he could not live up to the job and was eased out within the year and given an annual allowance to keep him in a manner that would not shame the family. He then lived in Paris where, unable to pay his gambling creditors, he sold off his interests in the bank, once again severing the Stourhead/Hoare's Bank connection.

There were no more children after those first two years of marriage. To add to Augusta's miseries, their son Charles, the future heir to Stourhead and the title after his spendthrift father, was at aged four unable to speak or walk and labelled, as was the case in those days, an 'idiot'. He died in France in 1854, at only seven years old, and was buried at Sablonville near the Bois de Boulogne. There is a large portrait of Augusta in the Hall at Stourhead, made in 1858, four years after Charles' death by her friend, the Victorian classical painter Lord Leighton, in which she appears in mourning black, pale and sad. But perhaps the resignation in those eyes is due as much to her difficult marriage as to the loss of her son, left behind in France since her husband, now *Sir* Henry Ainslie, had inherited Stourhead in 1857 and they had moved back to England. He would be master of Stourhead for 37 years, but for him it was a sporting estate, not a home.

There were attempts at looking after Stourhead in those first few years. Pictures were cleaned and varnished, and general repairs made indoors. The wooden bridge by the Pantheon was now replaced in iron (or was that his sensible agent Robert Shackleton choosing not to throw good money after bad?). He made a fountain for Augusta on the west side of the house, which she turned into a dogs' graveyard.

There were further trees added to the garden that were newly introduced to Europe, and again one wonders at whose instigation they reached Stourhead. There were more of those 'cedars': one was the silvery blue-leaved form of the (real) Atlas cedar, *Cedrus atlantica* 'Glauca', from the Atlas mountains of North Africa. Another was the so-called Japanese cedar, *Cryptomeria japonica*, the tree seen as massive, ancient specimens in so many Japanese temple shrines, and again with soft bark, if not as spongy as that of the

RIGHT Augusta, Lady Hoare (d.1903) mourning the loss of her young son, painted by Lord Leighton, 1858.

redwoods. Also from Japan came the Sarawa cypress, *Chamaecyparis pisifera*, and the hiba, *Thujopsis dolabrata*.

Still, it seemed as if Ainslie's habits were not likely to change and a mutual indifference grew between him and Augusta. He spent most of his life either in Paris or at one of their various London houses such as the one in fashionable Eaton Place, convenient for the Houses of Parliament, where he briefly became the (Liberal) Member for Windsor, and then between 1866 and 1874 the Member for Chelsea, after which he defected to the Tories. As was the practice in those days, fresh produce was regularly supplied to Eaton Place from Stourhead's kitchen garden.

Sometimes accompanied by Henry Ainslie, Augusta and Gussy would spend the summer and autumn at Stourhead, and then for the winter would move either to London or Paris. A portrait of Gussy (1860) also painted by Lord Leighton shows her at 14 years old. In 1868 Gussy married William John Nettleship Angerstein of Weeting, Norfolk. His German émigré family had arrived in England from Russia in the early eighteenth century and became rich as founders of Lloyd's insurance. Their collection of pictures was later acquired to become the core of the British National Gallery. But it seems to have been a family of bankrupts including, in 1880, Gussy's husband who was, according to court records, a 'Gentleman of no Occupation'. Not surprisingly, Gussy and her four children spent a good deal of time with their grandmother Augusta at Stourhead. For Augusta these were her happiest

of times; how different Stourhead must have seemed with young children there again, picnicking or riding through the woods.

In political circles Henry Ainslie was now a Tory and was keen to support the Primrose League when it was set up in 1883. Its aim was to encourage the working classes towards Conservatism, and in its efforts for membership it soon outnumbered the trade unions, partly because it allowed women to be members. Henry Ainslie spoke at public meetings for the League, and the organisation survived right through the twentieth century, only closing in 2004. Margaret Thatcher wrote for its *Gazette* in 1977.

But a gambling habit rarely goes away, and the 1870s and 1880s saw a serious agricultural depression in Britain, which reduced dramatically the income from an estate like Stourhead. It became necessary for Henry Ainslie to capitalise some of his assets in order to pay his debts. Although it needed an Act of Parliament to break the Trusts Colt Hoare's will had established, in 1883 a great sale was held, in which many of the more important family heirlooms were sold. Among them were a number of the better paintings, including Poussin's *Rape of the Sabines*, Turner's *Lake Avernus* and his drawings of Salisbury Cathedral so praised by Colt

LEFT Augusta's daughter Gussy, aged fourteen, painted by Lord Leighton, 1860.

RIGHT Agapanthus blooming in the gardens around the house.

Hoare. The portraits of the garden that Colt Hoare had commissioned from Francis Nicholson were also sold, as was his extensive collection of topographical books.

In 1885 Ainslie stood for Parliament again, as Conservative for East Somerset, but failed to gain the seat. Meanwhile the Third Reform Act effectively expanded the number of those eligible to vote to 60 per cent of the (male) population, meaning fewer voters were under the direct influence of a local landed candidate such as himself. It was a turning point for him. He left Stourhead immediately, never to return alive. He tried to let Stourhead but failed to find a suitable tenant, after which the house was closed – mothballed – although he stopped short of selling it, and retired to France, gout-ridden, where he died nine years later. He was buried at Stourton church.

# Autumn at Stourhead

Over the years, I have gained a true appreciation for the natural phenomenon that is autumn in the UK: the glorious motorway plantings that, in places, have been made with real landscape appreciation; individual trees that shine like beacons; trees and shrubs in various arboreta that I have visited have all contributed to my admiration for this annual festival of nature's beauty.

Stourhead was to top them all – the combination of landscape design, perfection in the scale and distribution of architecture, the deep reflections in the shimmering lake, and a tree collection from most corners of the world towering above the undulating garden floor below. During my first autumn at Stourhead in 1996 I can recall mornings when I headed into work feeling quite overwhelmed by the magnificence of the garden. Wondering if this was to be a one-off, perfect autumn I followed my mother's example, gathered some thick telephone directories and began to press some leaves. I never thought this display could be replicated in the future, so I wanted to record it in the best way possible. I collected leaves all through the garden's transition

LEFT  Every year the vibrant beauty of autumn fills the garden with colour and excitement.

from autumn to winter and then, in early December, they were dry. I had gathered hundreds of leaves from all across the garden and carefully pressed them to help them maintain their natural shape. I knew that I would not manage to capture their colour perfectly, and that they would fade to various shades of rust through to dark chocolate-brown, but that mattered not. During the dark evenings of December I placed each leaf carefully on a sheet of hard cardboard, overlapping the leaves with one another and building depth into the creation; some of the colour had faded a little, but it was still a reminder of the magic of the previous months' spectacle. Eventually I framed it and it hangs on my wall today; 23 years later I still have my first Stourhead autumn – it was my way of photographing it.

Autumn is not a single day, it is not just a week, it is an entire season. I am often asked when is the best time to see the garden during the autumn. If I am being honest it is usually the last week of October. However, to really appreciate the autumnal spectacle a few visits are definitely required. To put autumn into context you really need to start during the previous winter: to try to recall the silhouettes of the naked trees in the landscape; to visualise the grey skies that December is so good at delivering; and then to feel the hope when the first snowdrop punches its fragile head through the soil. Witnessing the onset of growth, the plant kingdom bursting into life, and the chorus so well practised by the birds during spring is truly a privilege. Everyone needs to allow the wonder of spring into their lives and appreciate the magnificent transformation that takes place when our landscape comes to life. The whole garden at Stourhead feels electric with nature's energy during springtime and this really is the start of preparation for autumn.

The efforts laid down during the early months of the year and through the long summer days are all part of the plants' natural progress through the seasons. By the time the days really begin to shorten in September, most plants will have completed their cycle of growth, flowering, going to seed and aspiring to reproduce. It is the shortening days, the reduction in available light, which begins to trigger the plants' autumn switches: sugars are extracted from the leaves; chlorophyll, the green pigment used for photosynthesis, is no longer needed as the days reduce in length, so it fades away and reveals the plethora of underlying colours in the leaves. Abscission layers begin to form at the base of the leaf stalks to allow for the clean separation of the leaf from the plant once every last drop of nutrition has been extracted. In essence, the leaves are beginning to die on the trees and shrubs.

The collection at Stourhead hails from many corners of the world and each species responds to the seasons here in different ways, which helps to add to the spectacle and lengthen the performance in the garden.

RIGHT Intelligent planting positions over 100 years ago help to create the display we see today.

Trees can be seen showing a hint of colour in August and others will be in full autumnal glory in November.

To me, spring feels like an announcement: it is nature's voice singing and shouting as it bursts into life and shares its excitement of the seasons ahead. Autumn, on the other hand, is a celebration of the seasons that have gone before. We felt the cold of winter, the days lengthening in spring and the first warmth of the sun on our skin; we smelt the scent of the flowers on the wind and the unique smell of rain on the breeze during summer. With the arrival of autumn, we are witnessing the crescendo of a busy year for the natural environment around us and we should all pause a few times to admire the natural fireworks in our gardens.

Stourhead is a living work of art. Standing back and admiring the magic of autumn, I feel like a spectator or an art critic studying a masterpiece; my eyes are busy and my mind is quickly absorbing the detail of what is in front of me. It is like reading a history book in a matter of seconds, correcting it as I read and noting down the areas for improvement. Many of the special moments in autumn come as I am driving in my car and I spot a beautiful tree in the distance or see a spectacular group of trees on the skyline, but what makes it all the more special at Stourhead is that I can step into the garden and explore every detail of this masterpiece.

LEFT The trees are the paint colours that bring this scene to life and keep this work of art ever changing and enchanting.

# Sir Henry Hugh Arthur Hoare

## *(1865-1947)* and Alda

# Victorian Innovation

Surely Stourhead was by now due for another safe pair of hands? In fact, it was rewarded with two when Henry Hugh Arthur and his wife Alda arrived to take over after Hugh Ainslie's demise in 1894. At 29 years old, Hugh Arthur was much younger (40 years) than his cousin Hugh Ainslie, and destined to be the last private owner of Stourhead, caring for it for 53 years. He and Alda stoically saw the estate through good and terrible times. For the garden, it was the third and last great period of its development.

The couple arrived in 1895 with their eight-year-old son, Harry, during a cold February, to a house that had been closed and dust-sheeted for nine years. They had every intention of making Stourhead a home again and for that it would have to be brought up to date. Income from the estate and Henry's directorship of Lloyd's Bank would facilitate this. For her part, Alda was business-like and tough, as photographs and paintings of her show: every bit the Edwardian lady, narrow-waisted, head held more than high, as if leaning back to take in a room full of new people.

For the duration of the refurbishment they lived in a house on the estate christened 'The Cottage', and meanwhile at Stourhead the shutters were opened and work began. Central heating delivered by hot water pipes began to be installed. The telephone arrived. Perhaps most significantly, the furniture and paintings from Henry's old home, Wavendon in Buckinghamshire, were brought to Stourhead with a view to letting the other house. Stourhead became happily cluttered in late Victorian fashion, as can clearly be seen in photographs of the house. Parlour palms and pots of lilies and cut flowers adorned every surface. It was happy, if fussy, and a million miles from the austere masculinity of Colt Hoare's scholarly imagination, although it was no doubt popular with the visiting public who were allowed in once more, between 2.30 and 6pm on Wednesdays.

There was plenty of activity in the garden. The Bristol High Cross, tottering and ready to fall, was repaired just in time, and all the temples and The Convent restored to good order. The Grotto had its usual periodic de-infestation from Colt Hoare's rampant laurels. The now-unfashionable 'eyesore' conservatory attached to the corner of the house was demolished and in the kitchen garden walls were repaired and the heating improved. The old vinery became a peach house and 118 new fruit trees were purchased. By a charming coincidence of interest, Harry Hoare, a cousin at the bank and another keen gardener, published two gardening books, *A Handbook on Flowering Trees and Shrubs* and *Spadework: or how to start a flower garden* (both 1902).

There was major clearance of Colt Hoare's rhododendrons, which like the laurels had run wild,

PREVIOUS PAGE  Like fall colour in New England, autumn colour at Stourhead is a gradual affair, progressing through the different species of tree until all the leaves have dropped and only leafless masses and the evergreen conifers remain.

RIGHT  Stourhead acquired its fair share of Victorian clutter – potted plants, endless chairs, velvet and frills. Clockwise from top left; Library, Cabinet Room, Music Room and Gallery.

ABOVE AND RIGHT Henry and Alda brought spring colour into the garden, with the notable addition of daffodils (above) and (right) laburnum. The pairing of purple beech and golden laburnum can be seen in thousands of nineteenth-century gardens.

filling the open spaces. In their place trees were planted, Douglas firs and noble firs and walnuts. Typically for the times, sombre purple beeches and golden laburnums came in, the beeches gradually making a massive and permanent change to the summer treescape through the many sudden contrasts they made between reflecting green and dark absences. With Henry and Alda, colour arrived in spades. No surprise, then, that to precede the golden laburnums thousands of daffodils were planted.

But then disaster struck. On the morning of 16 April 1902, fire gutted all but the two outer wings of the house. At 9am a housemaid had entered No.1 bedroom to find it full of smoke. It was that classic destroyer of old houses – a chimney fire – in which timbers may smoulder out of sight for days before finally catching light. Sir Henry, at a Lloyd's meeting in Salisbury, was called home at once, but by the time he arrived at 1pm the whole place was in flames and the central part of the house, Good Henry's original Palladian mansion, was effectively lost. The fire had been too well-established before it became apparent and water pumping systems were totally inadequate. Henry could only watch as the roof fell in.

# Rebuilding for the Modern Age

To everyone's credit there had been a huge effort to remove the house's contents before the fire reached the ground floor. Furniture was rushed outside, including the famous Pope's Cabinet, and Gainsboroughs and Poussins cut from their frames, while police constables stood guard over this rich salvage in the park. Mercifully, it was a dry day. At one point the fire started to find its way into the section that connected the main house to Colt Hoare's library wing, but it was successfully extinguished.

Paintings were lost on the stairs along with many fine and valuable mantlepieces, together with all the Chippendale bedroom furniture. On the top floor the servants had lost everything.

But Henry was no fool. Having made his refurbishments to the house he had immediately had it revalued for insurance at a solid £40,000, although in the end this turned out to be far from adequate to cover the restoration. Henry, Alda and the teenage Harry returned to the Cottage, but they were undaunted: in two months the basements were being revaulted as work began. In those days there was no legislative protection for even the best country houses, only for truly ancient ruins, and so they were free to rebuild as they thought appropriate, and this turned out, internally, to be largely a re-creation of the original house but with mod cons and better bedrooms that would give the house a more promising long-term future as a home. It was an opportunity to make real improvements that might not otherwise have been contemplated.

Henry chose to employ the local Salisbury architect, Doran Webb, who was already known to him. The main house we see today owes much to his design, though for Henry his employment became an expensive mistake.

After the fire, the west front was unstable and needed to be completely demolished, which was a chance to make the greatest of Webb's external changes. Before the fire, the façade had protruded heavily in the centre where Henry the Magnificent and his mother had pushed out the great saloon/dining room with a rather overbearing pediment. Doran Webb extended the façade still further, by adding on not to the centre but to each

ABOVE LEFT AND RIGHT Henry's original central block of the mansion was effectively burnt out in the fire of 1902, but Colt Hoare's two wings narrowly escaped the flames. Furniture and paintings were dragged out onto the lawn on what was a mercifully dry day. Fortunately the house was well insured.

corner, so that now the centre of the façade became recessed instead of protruding. A large, central staircase led down from it into the garden, as it once had on the south side before Colt Hoare removed it.

Behind that façade Webb made his greatest internal change. The ceiling of Henry the Magnificent's great saloon was lowered to make space for new bedrooms, which looked out from the centre of that new west front towards the obelisk. The original single staircase at the centre of the house was made double to accomodate this. The saloon was now less grand but also far less cavernous and no doubt much warmer.

There were valuable minor improvements: proper central heating, electric light and servants' bells powered from a generating house, decent plumbing and (no surprise here) fire hydrants and hoses installed throughout the house, fed from a 150,000-gallon (over 68,000 litre) water tank pumped by a petrol engine.

So far so good, but on a practical level Webb's work was less than satisfactory. By July 1905 Henry and Alda had begun to move back in and immediately found the house 'noisy', with sound passing uncomfortably loud between floors. There were also problems with flues, the very last thing Henry would have hoped for after a fire. To add to their problems their beloved son Harry was diagnosed with heart problems and for his better health was taken to Egypt for two months. A more experienced architect was called in, Sir Aston Webb (no relation), famous for his work at the Victoria and Albert Museum and the main buildings and tower of the University of

Birmingham. Aston Webb pronounced that the floors ought to have been 'double-joisted' and it became necessary to remake them at great expense, requiring yet another return to the Cottage. Alda took on the delicate business of telling Doran Webb what was required of him to make good. After a ten-minute interview she said, 'I was not out of temper but firm' and he left 'without Adieu'. Doran Webb resigned, and Aston Webb took over the whole project, completing it in 1906. Perhaps Doran Webb was better out of the way before it came to the handling of interior style (two men would spend a year hanging pictures and restoring furniture). Of Stourhead's over-furnished look, Doran Webb said with Wildean wit, 'Having been fortunate enough to get the things burnt, I cannot conceive anyone going out of their way to put the things back.'

LEFT The Italian Room, one of the bedrooms reconstructed by architect Doran Webb following the devastating fire of 1902.

RIGHT Webb's new west front, with extensions pushing forward on each corner of the façade and bold steps down into the garden.

# Garden Improvements

Work to the garden steamed ahead, while in 1907 young
Harry went off to Trinity College, Cambridge, to study.
Some of the temple statuary was moved to the house.
The lawn running down to the water in front of the
Pantheon was cleared of rhododendrons. Three
hundred azaleas came from Longleat, the Wiltshire
home of the Marquess of Bath. The islands in the lake
were cleared of scrub and self-sown trees, to be replaced
by today's tall tulip trees. New tree species of all kinds
found their way in. Some, like the Algerian fir and
Mediterranean stone pine, were only doubtfully hardy,
so plainly Henry was experimenting with his planting.
Some were fancy or dwarf varieties of species already
present in the garden, such as the golden-leaved
'Crippsii' form of the Japanese Hinoki cypress,
*Chamaecyparis obtusa*. Others were just out-and-out
ornamental varieties, like the brightly variegated form
of the sweet chestnut (there are ordinary green ones
in the park today which are 600 years old) and a new
grey-green shade found its way into the garden in the
form of eucalyptus trees. By the water weeping willows
added a new dynamic to the scene. More azaleas
came in together with the popular hardy hybrid
rhododendrons, bred, selected and named for their

RIGHT  It is a great tradition in British gardens that statues are a movable
feast. Many were moved to the house from the garden, for practical as
well as aesthetic and security reasons.

FAR RIGHT  Japanese maples, glowing red beside the water in autumn,
are much loved by artists and photographers.

LEFT *Henry Colt Arthur Hoare*, painted by St George Hare in 1909. He would have inherited Stourhead, had he not died in the First World War.

RIGHT *Sir Henry Hoare*, last owner of Stourhead who gave it to the National Trust in 1946. St George Hare, c.1909.

bright, distinct colours and flower size. (Such varieties were then most commonly grafted onto rootstocks of the common purple *Rhododendron ponticum*, the same one that Colt Hoare had introduced, so care had to be taken with the new hybrids that their rootstocks did not sprout from below, overwhelming the grafted plant and spreading yet more seed of the invasive *ponticum*.) More than ever, the garden was becoming a serious plant collection as well as a landscape.

Alfred's Tower was dangerously showing its age and urgently required repair since it was open to the public, but vandalism in 1907 – throwing stones at the bust of Alfred – led Henry reluctantly to close it. Further vandalism a few years later led to the closure of the garden altogether except by written permission.

In 1909 there was a big party at Stourhead to celebrate Harry's coming of age and his portrait was painted by St George Hare, who also painted his father and mother; the portraits of Sir Henry and Lady Hoare still hang in the Entrance Hall at Stourhead. Harry is shown leaning casually against a window with a cigarette, slightly plump, dressed palely, preoccupied as one might imagine a student to fancy himself. When he graduated in 1910, in recognition of his established commitment to the estate he was made Agent, in charge of its daily management. Modernisation continued in his care. Garages replaced stables, and were heated so that cars would start easily.

Alda became a friend and regular correspondent of the Wessex novelist Thomas Hardy and in due course a

friend of both his wives. He came to stay at Stourhead in 1914, and Alda collected his novels.

It might sound as if all was set fair for Stourhead, and that at last the estate would pass comfortably from one generation to the next, but relentless financial changes were afoot. Strange though it may seem today, income tax was only introduced in 1799 to help pay for the war against Napoleon, and even then it was for only a few years, although it was reintroduced in 1841. Of course, it was unpopular with the great estates, but at least they held political sway and had influence on the law.

# Financial Struggles

To cope with a £4 million government deficit, an inheritance tax on the capital value of land – death duty – was introduced in 1894, a Liberal measure hated by the Tories who saw it as an attack on the land-owning classes and great estates. Two deaths in close succession could cripple an estate. This meant that land, Henry the Magnificent's great trophy, was becoming a liability as well as an asset. With this in mind, and owning land in six counties, Henry Hugh began to sell, and Wavendon House itself, then let, was given major repairs with a view to selling it.

When war came in 1914 Harry immediately joined the Dorset Yeomanry. In his portrait, again painted by St George Hare, there is now a very different young man, serious and earnest in uniform. Knowing their son was out there fighting for King and Country, Henry and Alda gave their time generously to looking after wounded soldiers who were at home recuperating in the local

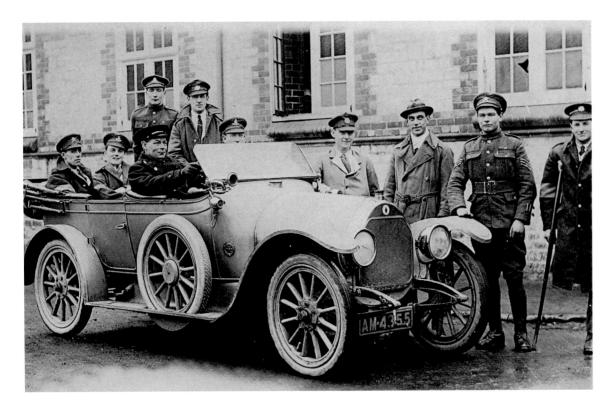

LEFT Lady Hoare encouraged foot-soldiers and officers recuperating in the hospital in Mere to visit Stourhead.

RIGHT Looking west to the Sun Pillar, past Urania (Ourania), the muse of astronomy.

hospital in Mere. Alda's 'Dear Tommies' would be driven to Stourhead for the afternoon, to be shown the house and pictures, given a slap-up tea and afterwards there might be music or a chance to fish the lake.

Harry fought at Gallipoli in the Dardanelles but succumbed to pneumonia and paratyphoid, for which he was repatriated to Stourhead, returning to the field as soon as he was fit again. In Palestine in November 1917 he was shot through the lungs in the Battle of Mughar Ridge and remained on the field all night before being brought in the next day. He died of heart failure a few days later in hospital in Alexandria. Yet again, Stourhead had been cheated of its heir. 'Our only and the best of sons,' wrote his father in the Annals. 'He never grieved us by thought, word or deed. He loved Stourhead, worked for it, and with us, all his life. He was deeply respected by all here who mourn his loss.'

Still Henry and Alda did not give up hope for their beloved Stourhead though even tougher times lay ahead. The sale of Wavendon brought in £45,000 and the Brewer estate £25,000. But by the 1920s financial pressures on large houses were even greater, and after the slaughter of the war, staff were harder to find. Houses were widely being sold, yet at Stourhead there was merely consolidation and a drawing in of horns.

RIGHT Darkness descends first on the world of ancient Rome, then the Renaissance bridge, and finally the Gothic Cross and living village. In the morning civilisation dawns with Rome.

Through the 1930s, perhaps as a solace though wondering what would become of Stourhead after their deaths, Henry continued to plant in the garden. There were rhododendrons still, classic varieties like 'King George', 'Tally Ho' and 'Mrs G.W. Leak', but also elegant Japanese maples and cherries with rich autumn colours, and magnolias to freshen the spring, together with ever more unusual firs, spruces and pines. A fernery was made. The Temple of Apollo was deemed ready to collapse and its lead roof replaced by a new Ruberoid compound instead of more expensive lead.

But in the face of increasing property taxes, owners not just of land but of unwanted and difficult-to-run great houses began literally to pull them down and to retreat to the most manageable and convenient of their properties. The newspaper *The Bystander* wrote in 1931:

*'The landed classes are, in fact, being taxed out of existence under our very noses and before our very eyes. It is one of the most dramatic and cruel episodes in the whole of England's chequered career, and most people who should know better talk like the Socialists and say that it is all for the public good. They forget that England became what she is as a result of the feudal system and that the feudal system is the best possible thing for the countryside. Time and time again in the past great landlords used to remit the rent to their tenants if it was a bad year. They were able to see that tenants got proper attention if they were ill. In fact, they looked after them. Today there is no one to do that. There is no doubt about it that the politicians have got the country into such a position that there is practically no chance for any great estate to survive financially the death of two consecutive heads of the family. It might be possible if there were a couple of very long minorities. But that is the only hope. In fifty years' time who can say with any assurance if a single one of the great houses will still be in private hands?'*

Even Stowe, that cradle of the landscape garden, barely escaped the squeeze. Its owner, the Duke of Buckingham, was declared bankrupt in 1848 and sold the contents, but it was not a full solution. It was sold in 1921 to a philanthropist who intended to give it to the nation, but the government would not take it without an endowment that he could not afford to give, and so in 1922 a final sale saw off every last object indoors and out, and the house was sold to the governors of what would become today's Stowe School. With difficulty the garden was respectably maintained but passed to the National Trust in 1989.

Then came the next war of 1939–45. Of course, Henry and Alda did what they could for the country. The Devonshire Regiment arrived at Stourhead in 1940; 20 officers billeted in the house, the men in the stables and Memorial Hall. It was a wicked winter, with temperatures of -14°C (25°F). They installed a fuel-gobbling AGA cooker. In 1941 Henry reluctantly gave permission for the temporary airfield RAF Zeals to be set up on the estate. The conical roof turret of Alfred's tower was sliced off one foggy day in July 1944 by a plane containing five American airmen coming in to land. Tragically, all were killed.

# Plans for the Future

Henry was now almost 80 and the future of Stourhead had to be decided. He had watched as the Portman family at Bryanston in Dorset had suffered six successive deaths in 29 years, bringing them to their knees financially through inheritance tax. In 1925 there was a 14-day sale of the contents and the house was shut up empty for several years before being sold, again as a school. Henry found it appallingly sad, impersonal and degrading. So what should he do?

He considered leaving Stourhead to the bank, as a sporting retreat, with one of the partners living there. Or he might leave it to the bank but require that, if they needed to sell, the proceeds would go to a specified hospital. He could leave it to the nation, but the nation had no great experience of caring for houses, and they too might just sell it. Then he thought of the National Trust for Places of Historic Interest or Natural Beauty, founded in 1895 at the time they themselves were coming to live at Stourhead: that could be the solution.

LEFT Tazzas stand each side of the front door, gripped by eagles that represent the Hoare crest.

# Stourhead and the National Trust

## (1946–present)

# In Safe Hands

If Henry were to give Stourhead to the National Trust it would achieve two goals: to ensure the preservation of both his beloved house and garden; and to avoid paying onerous inheritance tax on the value of the estate. The Trust had been founded in 1895 for 'The preservation for the benefit of the nation of lands and tenements (including buildings) of beauty or historic interest and, as regards lands, for the permanent preservation of their natural aspect, features, and animal and plant life'. In 1937 the preservation of furniture, pictures and chattels of any description having national and historic or artistic interest was added to the National Trust Act and in the same year the creation of the Country Houses Scheme made it possible for the Trust to accept estates and houses with their contents. This turn of events allowed Sir Henry to find a solution to his difficulties, and the National Trust seemed like a natural fit. At the time, the Trust did not own as much land or property as it does today although, significantly, it was negotiating for Lawrence Johnston's house and garden at Hidcote Manor in the Cotswolds. When Hidcote was accepted in 1948 it would become the organisation's first garden to be shown as a stand-alone attraction with no house, and as such it was a seminal step forwards (the house was kept closed for Johnston's use and not seen at all).

The years before and after the 1939–45 war were the time when the National Trust acquired many of its large houses and gardens. In those early days, the Trust was a tiny organisation, run rather like a club by a small number of highly motivated, influential, aristocratic

PREVIOUS PAGE If all too few Hoare children lived to enjoy Stourhead, it is enjoyed by countless children today. It is one of the National Trust's most visited gardens.

ABOVE James Lees-Milne, diarist and secretary to the National Trust's Country House Committee, helped negotiate a generous deal with Sir Henry for the Trust to take Stourhead.

RIGHT Hidcote Manor was taken on by the National Trust in 1948, the first to be accepted because of its garden.

LEFT Sir Henry and Lady Alda on their Silver Wedding in 1912, she with her usual corseted Edwardian glamour and tilted-back stance. Harry stands between them.

RIGHT Would Henry the Magnificent recognise this view at first glance, now filled with different tree species and shrubs?

or well-to-do enthusiasts, with a tiny professional staff. Handing over a grand family property to the Trust at that time, however painful, must have felt at least a little like giving it to careful, sensible friends rather than to a public charity.

The man in charge of vetting new properties for the Trust was James Lees-Milne, acting as secretary (1936–50) to the Trust's Country House Committee. Lees-Milne's wife Alvilde was the lover of Vita Sackville-West, who was instrumental in Hidcote coming to the Trust; Lees-Milne would later become the first biographer of Vita's husband Harold Nicolson who, with Vita, made the garden at Sissinghurst Castle in Kent, one day also to pass to the Trust and stand with Hidcote and Stourhead amongst its most visited gardens. So small still is the world of gardening.

Lees-Milne kept a diary and in later life he published *Ancestral Voices*, which included personal and perhaps self-mockingly waspish accounts of his visits to the owners of properties on offer to the Trust. His visit to see Henry and Alda, staying overnight at Stourhead, pleased him greatly:

> '*Sir Henry is an astonishing nineteenth-century John Bull, hobbling on two sticks. He was wearing a pepper and salt suit and a frayed grey billycock over his purple face … Lady Hoare is an absolute treasure, and unique. She is tall, ugly and eight-two … She has a protruding square coif of frizzy grey hair in the style of the late nineties, black eyebrows and the thickest spectacle lenses I have ever seen. They are the dearest old couple. I am quite in love with her outspoken ways and funny old-fashioned dress.*'

Henry took him on a tour of the garden in a great loop around the lake, he in his powered buggy, half-pram, half-motorbike, and Lees-Milne trotting along behind.

A deal went through. The Trust would have the house and its contents plus 1,072ha (2,650 acres) of the estate, including its income. In return, Henry's heir – a cousin, Henry Peregrine Rennie Hoare – and

subsequently his heirs would be able to live in the house rent-free, but the Trust would be able to open it to the public at agreed times. The transfer was made in 1946 and Henry and Alda, by extraordinary coincidence, died of old age on the same day a year later. He died in the afternoon and she in the evening, six hours later, unaware of his death. Rennie and his young family then moved in. In 1956 the family's regular accommodation

was reduced to an apartment, but with the Trust's help Stourhead continued to have an occasional social role. At the other end of the village, in Stourton House, formerly a rectory, lived Anthony Bullivant, an ebullient old soldier who was also making a garden that would become famous for its hydrangeas: with his help, hunt balls were held at Stourhead, but with 'no drink other than champagne, to avoid stains.'

# The Trust's Work Begins

Since the deal included so much accompanying land, the Trust was effectively being given a financial endowment with which to care for Stourhead. It was generosity indeed. In those days when the Trust was taking on great houses this was not always so, but such was its desire then to save great treasures for the nation that properties were accepted anyway. Today, in times when the Trust has much broader commitments and responsibilities, such houses cannot be taken on without adequate accompanying endowment.

With the garden in new hands, work began. It is in the nature of all old men's gardens that there is a good deal of over-mature planting that has been retained to avoid disturbance and will become the work of the next generation, which in this case was the National Trust. In particular, there was woodland work to be done, both in the garden and on the estate. The year 1953 saw a severe gale which produced huge numbers of fallen trees, a problem in itself but also, like all major clear-outs, a chance to make anew, and so in the place of planting that had become very mixed, there was a return to the beech so enjoyed by Henry the Magnificent, and which did so well locally. Views were opened up which had been lost for years. Paths were remade.

The Trust's Chief Gardens Adviser at this time was Graham Stuart Thomas, who had also been heavily involved in the acquisition of Hidcote. He took charge of much of the work at Stourhead and was keen to remove large areas of *Rhododendron ponticum* that had self-sown both into the open spaces and amongst the more deliberate plantings of brightly coloured hardy hybrid rhododendrons. He also made additions to the planting, choosing personally and pragmatically in the manner of Henry Hugh Arthur before him, from among flowering woodland trees and shrubs for spring and autumn colour. With help from the Historic Buildings Council, the dam and Rock Arch were restored. Yet again the roof of the Temple of Apollo was repaired, as it would be again in the present century.

LEFT The National Trust reopened the views at Stourhead and planted beech trees to replace trees that had blown down.

# Gardens for the Nation

If Stourhead had always been accessible to locals on open days and to the great and the good by appointment, what would happen now under Trust ownership which promised greater public access?

Here, one must understand the history of country-house gardens in the public consciousness. In the years after the Second World War there arrived the idea of the affordable family car, which transformed garden visiting because people could easily reach places that previously would have been too out of the way. The idea of a Sunday day out became commonplace. The National Gardens Scheme blossomed. As interest grew in visiting gardens for pleasure, so did an academic interest in gardens; in 1966 the Garden History Society was formed. In 1974 at the Victoria and Albert Museum in London, the director Roy Strong put on an exhibition entitled *The Destruction of the English Country House 1875–1975* followed shortly by *The Garden: A Celebration of a Thousand Years of British Gardening.* Gardening was becoming a serious and public affair. So it was that in 1973, after 17 years as a safe pair of hands and with pressure from Stourhead's great champion Kenneth Woodbridge, the Trust realised the need to develop a more dynamic approach to the garden at Stourhead.

A committee was formed to look at its past and future and how it should be managed. A report was produced in 1978, with the help of the Trust's Gardens Adviser John Sales. It was a seminal document in the care of historic gardens because it dealt, practically, with ways of looking at a garden which has passed from private hands, unconstrained by obligations to history, to the hands of a potentially impersonal and bureaucratic management system which was now, according to law, in place for all time, not just one person's lifetime. The report also begged questions about the nature of the Trust's opportunity to preserve or expand afresh the garden that the Hoares had handed over. It sounds an easy question. It is not.

RIGHT The island tulip trees, which miraculously survive and even thrive perched just above the water, form a middle ground to the views across the lake.

LEFT John Sales was Head of Gardens at National Trust and instrumental in the development and management of Stourhead.

Since that 1978 report even more has changed in the world of gardens. In 1983 the Register of Historic Parks and Gardens of Special Historic Interest in England was set up by government, effectively listing and grading gardens in the same way that buildings are listed. Along with listing came the requirement for their significance to be taken into account when planning alterations to gardens on the Register. A fashion for historic garden restoration took hold, not least as the new discipline of garden archaeology arrived on the scene and what was known *once* to have existed began almost to take precedence over what actually remained. There were major garden restorations such as the Privy Garden at Hampton Court Palace, which were famously strict in their adherence to historic precedent. At its most extreme, 'restoration as found' advocated putting nothing back at all which was no longer there – hardly restoration at all, some said, more a celebration of loss.

Other's took a freer approach, as exemplified by the Lost Gardens of Heligan in Cornwall, a garden restoration given huge amounts of publicity and air time because it presented itself as a moving tale of social history as much as a garden. Biddulph Grange, Staffordshire, made a splash in 1984 because it was a High Victorian plantsman's garden facing extinction.

Time marched on and by the 2000s strict restoration was starting to receive a bad press; it was regarded as 'sterile', uncaring, unambitious, interesting but soon boring. Attitudes began to swing in favour of a more flexible approach that would reflect and enhance the 'spirit of place' by preserving the best of what remained of the garden and being faithful to that, but which would still allow the development of those elements of the garden that were always intended to be dynamic and changing – colour schemes or plant collections or kitchen gardening.

# A Fresh Approach

Today it has become recognised, partly through the work of John Sales, that 'gardening is a process', by which it is meant that a garden is not planted, runs a course, dies, and then is started again. Rather it is like a ticking clock, a mechanism of interlocking and interdependent wheels, some turning faster than others. Trees turn on a scale of centuries; shrubs run on a scale of decades with buildings requiring repairs over the same time period; while perennial planting needs rejuvenating every few years, and bedding for colour is an annual process. It is the gardener's job to keep the whole clock ticking along as different plants grow and die. The repair of a living garden is an ongoing process; if a garden requires restoration then something has gone wrong.

The public today is sophisticated. There have been 40 years of unprecedented growth of interest in gardening. Garden visiting has boomed, as has membership of the Royal Horticultural Society (the RHS, scathingly known in the 1970s as the Rupture and Hernia Society because of the then average age of its modest number of members). Cheap colour printing in China revolutionised the process and full-colour gardening books abounded. Colour in newspaper printing meant the Saturday papers could carry pages of gardening. Magazines proliferated. With the advent of digital photography, everyone has become a photographer. BBC television's *Gardeners' World* gained huge audiences and the make-over series *Groundforce*, though it may have been a romp of a programme, allowed people who were new to gardening to think they could begin a garden without having studied horticulture at their grandmother's knee.

But far more important than all this, the post-war interest in gardens has meant that this country has now been able to afford, with occasional government and lottery help, to repair and restore gardens from every one of its historical periods and have them all in good condition concurrently, and able to be visited by people from all over the world. Gardeners have never had it so good. Such is the popularity of gardens. And people expect all gardens open to the public to be in excellent condition because they know what it looks like. The public has indeed become very sophisticated.

RIGHT It is the gardener's job to maintain the different plantings over years, decades and centuries.

# The Vision for Stourhead

What, then, did that seminal 1978 report propose for Stourhead 40 years ago? How did it propose it should be maintained, bearing in mind that it was already in sound condition? How should the Trust interpret and handle the intentions of the garden's creators to make Stourhead properly understood by the public? What has been done since, to meet present public expectations?

The report recognised that Stourhead is already a garden of many layers, one on top of another; a palimpsest, as fashionable terminology would have it. At the bottom is Henry the Magnificent's simple stylised landscape of green trees, grassy open space, water and temples. Over that is Colt Hoare's layer of denser, more diverse, romantic planting with less open space, together with his botanical collections under glass; and laid over that is the colourful plantsman's gardening of flowering trees and shrubs made in the twentieth century. All are valid elements of the garden and all of them mature at different speeds and require different frequencies of replanting.

In a multi-layered garden it is usually the most recent layer that is most conspicuous and most shapes one's abiding impression of it. But the Stourhead Report's proposal was not to let that happen, but to decide which parts of the garden best represented each phase of its development, and over the decades to lead these different areas back, broadly speaking, towards their original appearance. A compromise, yes, but setting out not to lose the vital distinctions between periods. The report was laying out priorities and aims, both long-term and short-term.

At the south end of the lake, therefore, where Henry's temples and water and clean vistas predominated, good trees which had been planted by his successors would be allowed to live out their lives but then not be replaced (this process continues today) so that Henry's simpler, greener landscape could rise closer to the surface and people might see what he intended – that fresh, simple, idealised landscape. At the top end of the lake where there had always been more plantsman's gardening, where maples and

LEFT  Reflections suggest a depth to the lake which is entirely absent in reality and yet the floating island trees also suggest the true shallowness. It is a delightful contradiction.

rhododendrons and azaleas and specimen conifers from the nineteenth and twentieth centuries predominate, that mix would not only continue to be maintained but be replanted.

There would be a need to accommodate the greater numbers of people visiting Stourhead, in particular by relocating paths so that there would not be a constant trail of people visible from the opposite bank of the lake. Large-scale parking must be carefully placed to prevent a tendency for visitors to walk the garden in reverse – they would need encouragement to resist that first captivating sight of the lake and to head instead to the house, so as to approach the garden from there as its owners intended.

There would have to be decisions, based partly on practicality and partly on cost, about replacing features such as the Chinese Umbrella and Turkish Tent and the tall-arched white Palladian bridge spanning the upper limb of the lake. By modern standards the bridge would be hazardous and therefore difficult to accommodate. It would also sit in the part of the garden intended to show more of the garden's later, plant-rich developments, not Henry's early, architecturally rich phase. And yet perhaps one day, when the tulip trees on the islands have lived their lives and the north end of the lake is exposed again, that would be the time to put back the bridge. Such are those interlocking wheels and long-term decisions; there must be logic and no hurry. Gardens take their time. Nor is any plan fixed forever. Circumstances change and there will doubtless

ABOVE Magnolias bring spring colour to Stourhead's population of smaller trees, followed later by towering rhododendrons. The high-canopy trees will outlive several generations of newly planted magnolias.

LEFT Paths must be carefully routed and surfaced to cope with increasing visitor numbers.

be adjustments. But having a plan in place certainly focuses the mind.

Meanwhile, in the walled garden, Richard Colt Hoare's idea of collecting fruit trees and pelargoniums under glass can thrive again. It is short-term gardening, the tiniest fast-moving wheel of the clock, for show, for the sheer pleasure of seeing the difference between species, to show plants for their own individual sakes rather than as part of a bigger outdoor picture.

Has a new sense of personality come to Stourhead through the National Trust? Probably not, but then perhaps Stourhead has more than enough layers of interest already. The work now has to be in carefully letting those layers speak distinctly without the garden becoming an argument, or simply babble.

People visit Stourhead today for many reasons; some to scrutinise the garden and its buildings, some to see that famous view or the autumn colour, some to walk the dog or stroll along the estate paths or see Alfred's Tower. Could Henry the Magnificent have guessed that his vision of Arcadia – his 'charming Gasp'd picture' – would speak so strongly to twenty-first century visitors? What would James Lees-Milne's sweet old couple have made of National Trust membership numbers rising from a few thousand to over 5 million? Or that half a million people would make the pilgrimage to see their garden every year? There is so much to be proud of at Stourhead for all involved, past and present.

# Further Reading

Barratt & Son, *Description of Stourhead* (1818)

Campbell, Colen, *Vitruvius Britannicus* (1715–25)

Colt Hoare, Richard, *Description of the House and Gardens at Stourhead, Salisbury* (1800)

Colt Hoare, Richard, *A Classical Tour Through Italy and Sicily* (1815)

Colt Hoare, Richard, *The History of Modern Wiltshire* (1830)

Colt Hoare, Richard, *The History of Ancient Wiltshire* (1812)

Gilpin, William, *Observations on the Western Parts of England* (1798)

Hoare, Harry, *A Handbook on Flowering Trees and Shrubs* (1902)

Hoare, Harry, *Spadework: or how to start a flower garden* (1902)

Hussey, Christopher, *The Gardens of Stourhead* (Country Life LXXX111, 1938)

Hutchins, Victoria, *Messrs Hoare Bankers: A history of the Hoare banking dynasty* (Constable, 2005)

Lees-Milne, James, *Ancestral Voices* (1975)

Palladio, Andrea, *The Four Books of Architecture* (1570)

Powys, Caroline, *Passages from the Diaries of Mrs Philip Lybbe Powys of Hardwick House* (1899)

Walpole, Horace, *Journals of Visits to Country Seats*

Wood, Robert, *The Ruins of Balbec* (1757)

Woodbridge, Kenneth, *Landscape and Antiquity: Aspects of English Culture at Stourhead 1718 to 1838* (Oxford, 1970)

Woodbridge, Kenneth, *The Stourhead Landscape* (The National Trust (booklet), 1970)

*The Conservation of the Garden at Stourhead: Report and Recommendations* (The National Trust, 1978)

# Picture Credits

Alamy Stock Photo © page 13 and 153 Kevin Dickinson; page 20 Artokoloro Quint Lox Limited; page 21 Peter Lane; page 30 R Vivian; page 32–33 Denis Chapman; page 36 Gary Cook; page 50 Steve Taylor ARPS; page 51 gardenpics; page 55 and 157 © colin chalkley; page 59 and 70 The National Trust Photolibrary; page 78 Neil Maclachlan; page 88 myLAM; page 114 Tim Ennis; page 115 and 116 © mauritius images GmbH; page 133 Steffen Hauser/botanikfoto; page 158 escapetheofficejob; page 161 Sashinax; page 162 David Hansford Photography; page 165 B Christopher.

National Trust Images © page 19, 22, 35, 58, 72–73, 93 left, 93 right, 134; page 2–3, 62, 63, 65 Andrew Baskott; page 4, 46, 47, 54, 56, 66, 110, 136, 145 James Dobson; front cover, page 7, 82–83, 125 Simon Tranter; page 8–9, 23 (3rd down), 85, 86, 90, 100, 119, 120, 137, 140 John Hammond; page 10 Timothy Smith; page 16–17, 24, 71, 91, 92, 112 Dennis Gilbert; page 23 top, 131 top left, 131 top right, 131 bottom left, 131 bottom right, 141, 142, 152 David Cousins; page 25 Bill Batten; page 26, 42, 48, 49, 67, 96, 121, 126, 128 Tamsin Holmes; page 29, 37, 74–75, 108–109, 164 Clive Nichols; 60, 107 Jerry Harpur; page 39 Solent News & Photography Agency; page 40, 41 Andrew Butler; page 44, 53, 94, 95, 122, 154 Brian & Nina Chapple; page 52 Katharine Davies; page 57 Dawn Biggs; page 61, 97, 113 Nick Mccrs; page 77 Stephen Robson; page 80 Anthony Parkinson; page 89, 138, 143, 147, 166 Arnhel de Serra; page 98, 103 Simon Knight; page 101 Abby George; page 104, 159 John Millar; back cover, page 132 Mark Bolton; page 135 John Bethell; page 139 Ian Shaw; page 148–149 Nick Daly; page 151 Sarah Davis.
National Trust © page 23 (2nd down) Sue James; page 150 Robert Thrift.

Page 68 © Tate, London 2019.
Page 69 © Copyright The National Gallery, London 2019.
Photograph page 111 by Sam Smith.
Photograph page 156 courtesy of the Sales family.

# Index

# Stephen Anderton

Stephen Anderton is a long-standing garden writer for *The Times* and international lecturer. Previously he worked in the care of historic gardens, latterly as National Gardens Manager for English Heritage, and was responsible for several major garden restoration projects in the north. His books include *Discovering Welsh Gardens*, the biography *Christopher Lloyd: His Life at Great Dixter*, and *Lives of the Great Gardeners*. He lives near Abergavenny in the Black Mountains and when not gardening writes music for the theatre.

# Alan Power

Alan Power has worked in some of the most beautiful gardens in the country, notably Mount Stewart in Northern Ireland as Head Gardener, Hidcote in Gloucestershire as Custodian Head Gardener and Stourhead in Wiltshire, arriving on the Garden team in 1996 and, after a period away at Mount Stewart, returning as Head Gardener in 2003. He has worked with the *Gardeners' World* team, presented on *British Gardens in Time* for BBC 4 and been a regular contributor on BBC Radio 4. Alan has lectured across Europe, in the US and in 2016 was presented with an Honorary Doctorate Degree from Writtle University.

# Mike Calnan

Mike Calnan is the National Trust's Head of Gardens – the professional lead for the Trust's gardens and gardening community, a role he has held for 21 years. His remit covers setting the overall direction for gardens, plant conservation and gardener training. His interests in gardens are wide ranging, though he has a particular fascination for eighteenth-century gardens and has advised on the restoration of many National Trust gardens from this period, including Berrington Hall, Stowe, Studley Royal and Petworth. Mike is also a specialist in the application of aerial photography to historic garden and landscape conservation.